performance appraisals

10

MINUTE

GUIDE

Macmillan USA, Inc.
201 West 103rd Street
Indianapolis, IN 46290

A Pearson Education Company

Dale Furtwengler

10 Minute Guide to Performance Appraisals

Contents

1   The Goals of Performance Appraisal   **1**

The Elements of Performance Appraisals 1
Performance Improvement 1
Employee Development 4
Employee Satisfaction 5
Compensation Decisions 6
Communication 8
The 30-Second Recap 8

2   Improving Performance   **9**

Measuring Performance 9
Current Performance 15
Desired Performance 15
The 30-Second Recap 18

3   Encouraging Employee Development   **19**

Becoming a Mentor 19
Evaluating Strengths 21
Exploring Employee Interests 22
Matching Strengths and Interests 24
The Need for a Development Plan 25
Creating a Development Plan 26
The 30-Second Recap 28

4   Striving for Employee Satisfaction   **29**

The Benefits of Having Happy Employees 29
What Makes Employees Happy? 35
Employee Differences 40
The 30-Second Recap 41

5   Compensating Employees   **42**

A Common Occurrence 42
Avoiding Problems 44

The Value Proposition 45
Base Pay 49
Incentive Compensation 50
The 30-Second Recap 51

6   **Improving Communication**   **52**
The Impact of Poor Communication 52
The Keys to Effective Communication 53
The Role of Communication in Performance Appraisals 61
The 30-Second Recap 64

7   **Looking at Sample Questions**   **65**
Appraisal Form Design 65
Performance 70
Other Evaluation Criteria 72
360° Feedback 77
The 30-Second Recap 78

8   **Three Approaches to Performance Appraisals**   **79**
Approach One: Favors the Evaluator 79
Approach Two: A Balanced Approach 79
Approach Three: Employee Participation 80
A Few Reminders 82
The 30-Second Recap 83

9   **Preparing for the Meeting**   **84**
Process Versus Project 84
Your Style 84
Employee's Style 87
Blending Styles 90
The 30-Second Recap 91

10 **The Meeting**   **92**
Factors Influencing Employee Comfort 92
Setting the Tone of the Meeting DCF 95
The 30-Second Recap 99

11 Gaining Your Employees' Trust 101

The Importance of Trust 101

Trust—Right or Privilege? 102

The 30-Second Recap 107

12 Forging Agreements 108

Levels of Agreement 108

Agreeing on Your Employee's Strengths 109

Discussing Improvement Opportunities 110

The 30-Second Recap 116

13 Feedback Systems and Recognition Programs 117

Feedback Systems—The Missing Link 117

Marketing 119

Sales 122

Production 123

Credit and Collection 123

Human Resources 124

Finance 125

Recognition Programs 127

The 30-Second Recap 128

14 You Can't Win 'Em All 129

The Problem 129

The Solution 133

The 30-Second Recap 138

15 Pulling It All Together 140

Performance Appraisal—A Process 140

Time Commitments 141

Establishing Time Frames For Corrective Action 143

The 30-Second Recap 146

A Glossary 147

B Further Readings 150

Index 151

Introduction

How does Jack Welch, the chairman and CEO of General Electric, spend most of his time at work? On strategy? He answered that question a few years ago in a television interview where he said, "I spend my time on people. If you have the right people, strategy takes care of itself."

On the surface it might appear that Mr. Welch is saying that you should devote your time and attention to recruiting. Certainly a well-conceived, properly implemented recruiting strategy will pay big dividends, but there is more to his message. I believe that Mr. Welch is telling you that your primary responsibility as a leader is the development of people.

You may have been hired for your finance, marketing, production, or technology skills, but you were promoted so that you can help others develop the skills that make you so successful.

Initially you may think, "That's not so difficult. I know my stuff. It'll be easy to teach others how to do what I do." Then you realize that your ability is only part of the equation. You need employees who possess

- Skills on which to build.

- The desire to learn.

- An ability to learn.

- A work ethic.

- Interest in the work that needs to be done.

- A desire to see the company succeed.

- The confidence to succeed.

Now you're wondering, "What did I get myself into?" Take heart! There's a tool to help you become a master at developing people. It's the performance appraisal.

This powerful tool enables you to assess all of the factors listed above and more. I'm sure some of you are wondering "If this tool is so wonderful, why do many supervisors dread its use?"

First, performance appraisals don't often come with complete, clearly written instructions. It's like trying to assemble your kids' toys. Even with instructions it's not a lot of fun.

Second, you know that during the appraisal meeting, you're going to tell the employee that he needs to improve. That's a pleasant thought!

Some managers tout the use of "constructive criticism" as a way to soften the message. Their belief is that the employee feels better knowing that the criticism is designed to help him. That's ridiculous! Criticism stings the ego. You know it and I know it.

There are ways to help employees improve performance without criticizing them. In this book, you'll learn techniques and language that will allow you to create a truly constructive and productive work environment, one in which your employees will flourish, and you'll be recognized as a master people developer.

CONVENTIONS USED IN THIS BOOK

This book makes use of three sidebars that help you find the information you need:

TIP

> Tips give you a different perspective on what has been said—to get you thinking.

PLAIN ENGLISH

> Plain English sidebars provide definitions of terms that might be new to you.

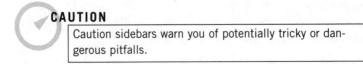

CAUTION

Caution sidebars warn you of potentially tricky or dangerous pitfalls.

ACKNOWLEDGMENTS

I would like to thank everyone who worked on this project. You know who you are—the book would not have been possible without you.

LESSON 1

The Goals of Performance Appraisal

In this lesson, you will learn about performance factors evaluated in the appraisal process so you can see exactly how powerful this tool is.

THE ELEMENTS OF PERFORMANCE APPRAISALS

Performance appraisals encompass

- Performance improvement.
- Employee development.
- Employee satisfaction.
- Compensation decisions.
- Communication skills.

An impressive array of performance factors, isn't it? Let's look at each more closely.

PERFORMANCE IMPROVEMENT

Performance is measured in terms of

- Speed.
- Quality.
- Service.
- Value.

These and other measures are becoming increasingly important in gaining and maintaining a competitive advantage. Most major companies already focus on these measures, and many require their vendors to do so as well. If you aren't tracking these items, here are some reasons why you should.

SPEED

We live in a world where companies achieve *mass customization* with just-in-time inventory systems.

Just-in-time inventory systems are designed to bring in only those materials needed for the current day's production. This allows the company to avoid expensive storage and handling costs. Some companies are so adept at just-in-time inventory that they now order material by the shift, rather than by the day.

PLAIN ENGLISH

> **Mass customization** is the process of customizing your product or service to meet the individual customer's need while serving thousands of customers every day.

Motorola employs both of these techniques. You can order five cell phones from Motorola, each with different features and colors, and receive delivery the next day. There are a lot of factors that influence Motorola's ability to achieve this speed:

- Salespeople need to place orders quickly.

- Materials must be ordered to arrive just in time.

- Vendors must deliver materials on time.

- The materials must be free of defects.

- Production personnel must assemble the phones efficiently.

- Shipping team has to choose a quick, reliable, cost-effective method for getting the order to the customer on time.

- The delivery company has to deliver on time.

This entire cycle from placing the order to delivering the finished product involves hundreds, if not thousands, of people whose performance must be quick and virtually error free.

This is just one example of why speed has become an important measure of performance.

QUALITY

Speed without quality is useless. If one of Motorola's vendors ships defective parts, the whole system fails. The customer is unhappy, additional pressure is put on the production schedule, and the costs of rework are formidable. No one wins. Quality is imperative in performance measures.

SERVICE

Ask anyone and you'll find that poor service (during or after the sale) will negate any benefits gained from speed and quality. This is as true of *internal customers* as it is with *external customers*.

PLAIN ENGLISH

> **Internal customers** are people within your organization who rely on you for service. **External customers** are people outside your organization whom you serve.

Some departments serve both internal and external customers. The accounting department provides financial information to operating managers who are internal customers. They also report financial results to external customers such as stockholders, bankers, and possibly the Securities and Exchange Commission.

VALUE

Customers have always demanded *value*. Does that mean they are always willing to pay for higher quality? See the following example to learn how a printer answered that question.

PLAIN ENGLISH

Value is the combination of quality and price that allows the buyer to feel that she's getting more than she is paying.

Most people can't tell the difference between a good print job and a great print job. Since the difference is imperceptible, most customers won't pay for a great print job. The key is the customer's perception of quality. If the customer can't see a difference in quality, she won't pay for it.

TIP

As you establish measures for use in performance appraisals, ask yourself, "Will an improvement in this measure be valued by the customer?"

These four criteria—speed, quality, service, and value—are the basis for judging your employee's performance. Once you've evaluated her current performance, you can help her develop an improvement plan.

EMPLOYEE DEVELOPMENT

This segment of the performance appraisal process deals with employee skills. What skills does the employee possess? What skills are needed for the future? Does the employee have enough background on which to build, or should she consider other career paths?

If the employee is capable of developing the skills, where can she get the appropriate training? Even if she can develop the necessary skills, does she possess enough interest in the work to want to develop those skills?

The answers to these questions are vital to your employee's success. The performance appraisal helps you carry out your role of mentor and coach. There is no greater calling than helping others become the best they can be. In order to do that, you must

- Clearly see your employee's strengths.

- Encourage her to improve.

- Provide insights and tools to help her improve.

- Celebrate her successes.

- Help her work through the difficult times.

Perform this role well, and you'll develop very successful employees who treasure your leadership. You'll also open the door for greater opportunities for yourself.

EMPLOYEE SATISFACTION

Have you ever tried to improve the performance of an unhappy employee? Root canals are more pleasant!

The performance appraisal can help you anticipate and often prevent employee dissatisfaction. It helps you uncover employee attitudes toward

- Variety.

- Growth.

- Challenge.

- Learning.

- Participation.

- Security.

- Autonomy.

- Money.

- Their own abilities.

In Lesson 4, "Striving for Employee Satisfaction," I discuss each of these factors and their impact on the employee's performance and job satisfaction. You'll also learn some techniques for anticipating and avoiding employee dissatisfaction. For now, I simply want you to know that changes in employee attitudes are precursors of changes in job satisfaction.

When I read news reports about employees quitting their jobs to take lower-paying jobs, I wonder whether the leaders were surprised when the employees gave notice. Don't allow yourself to be surprised by the loss of a good employee. Learn to read the signs of change.

TIP

> If you're not adept at reading body language, listening for verbal cues, or asking leading questions, add these to the list of skills you want to develop.

COMPENSATION DECISIONS

A few years ago one of my clients asked me to evaluate his bonus program. Here's the program: At the end of the year he would determine whether or not his company made any profit. If the company made money, he would decide what percentage to pay out in bonuses and to whom. In loss years, he didn't pay a bonus.

Rather than evaluate his program, I asked him to evaluate it from the employee's perspective. You may want to try this yourself.

You're a good employee. You're dependable, you require little supervision, you do quality work, and you even find some ways to become more productive. At the end of the year you get a bonus. You feel like you've earned it, right?

The following year, you continue to exhibit all the same traits, and you find even more ways to increase your productivity. The company loses money; you don't get a bonus. The explanation is that sales were off.

Now, unless you're responsible for sales, you're thinking, "It's not my fault that sales are down; I did my job. It's not fair to penalize me for someone else's failure." You're right! You shouldn't be penalized, yet it happens every day.

TIP

> Always tie your employees' compensation to quantifiable results. Then make sure that they can track their progress in generating results. That removes the element of surprise from salary reviews.

Another thing wrong with my client's system is that the employee doesn't know what to expect in the way of compensation. It's tough to stay motivated when the reward isn't obvious. Here's how you can use performance appraisals to avoid these problems:

- During the appraisal process you and your employee agree on performance and personal development goals.

- You also agree on future compensation for various levels of achievement.

- Finally, the two of you establish a tracking system that allows the employee to track her progress.

This simple approach makes future compensation decisions a foregone conclusion. As you can see, the performance appraisal is a wonderful tool for avoiding the headaches normally associated with salary reviews.

COMMUNICATION

In today's fast-paced world communication is suffering. I'd bet that most of you don't have time to communicate as fully as you once did. Yet communication is more vital than ever because the pace is so rapid.

When we get rushed, we forget to tell employees what we expect or, worse yet, we fail to let them know that they aren't meeting expectations. The appraisal's greatest value as a communication tool lies in its ability to help us determine where we aren't communicating as effectively as we should.

TIP

You can assure effective communication between performance appraisals by establishing communication triggers. These triggers are deadlines, events, or results that cause you and your employee to get together to evaluate performance and establish new goals. Communication triggers provide a sort of safety net to assure that neither you nor your employees are surprised during future appraisals.

THE 30-SECOND RECAP

Performance appraisals have the power to help you

- Improve employee performance.
- Develop your employees' skills for the future.
- Increase employee satisfaction.
- Make good compensation decisions.
- Improve communication with your employees.

LESSON 2
Improving Performance

In this lesson, you'll learn how to establish performance measures. You'll also learn about common mistakes associated with performance measures and how these measures promote continuous improvement.

MEASURING PERFORMANCE

The phrase *"performance measure"* is intuitively satisfying, yet frighteningly vague. Simultaneously, you feel comforted by the thought of being able to measure results and distressed by the prospect of having to create the measure. The key to avoiding this conflict lies in understanding how measures are created.

The natural tendency is to measure the end result. There are a couple of problems with this approach:

1. Not all results are measurable.

2. Other useful measures are overlooked.

NOT ALL RESULTS ARE MEASURABLE

Let's assume your goal is to improve employee morale. That's tough to measure. Sure, you can survey your employees before and after an initiative, but there are a lot of factors that influence morale besides your effort. One of the most important is your employee's frame of mind on the days surveyed.

Did the employee just fight with his spouse? How was traffic that morning? Are the kids ill? Did the car break down? Or did the employee wake up feeling that everything is right with the world? All these factors influence the employee's morale on the date surveyed. The presence of these external influences makes the value of the surveys suspect.

OTHER USEFUL MEASURES ARE OVERLOOKED

In recent years we've seen a dramatic increase in the use of *process mapping* and *activity-based costing* to define performance measures. Both tools are designed to identify redundancies and inefficiencies in systems and approaches.

PLAIN ENGLISH

Process mapping is a method used to examine the effectiveness of the current approach used in accomplishing a task. It's called process mapping because it provides a visual map of the various steps in a process. These steps are listed in the order performed, then analyzed with an eye to increasing efficiency.

PLAIN ENGLISH

Activity-based costing views all processes involved in offering a product or service to your customers. It looks at the costs of everything from marketing, through delivery, to the final paperwork. Activity-based costing even examines the costs of billing the customer, the cost of slow payment, and the cost of processing vendor invoices and payments to the vendors.

These powerful tools are excellent for generating ideas for improving performance and establishing performance measures.

One of the reasons these approaches are so effective is that they allow you to create smaller projects. While it may take years to achieve your end result, it often takes only days or weeks to improve a step in the process.

Each success moves your team closer to its overall goal. Each success intensifies the team's belief that it will be successful on a larger scale. The combination of these two elements, success and confidence, will accelerate the achievement of the result you seek.

Now that I've identified some worthwhile tools for creating measures, here are the hallmarks of effective performance measures. They must be

- Quantifiable.

- Easy to understand.

- Well balanced.

- Easy to track.

- Frequently published.

QUANTIFIABLE

You must be able to represent the measure numerically. Time, error rates, retention rates, units produced, absenteeism, cost, and profitability are all measures that lend themselves to numeric representation. Most can be adapted to a variety of operating situations.

For example, retention rates can be applied to both customers and employees. Error rates can be applied to manufacturing and administrative functions. Speed is as useful in measuring responsiveness to customers as it is in gauging the timeliness of information from the accounting department.

The key is that all these measures are quantifiable. They may be stated in percentages, actual performance numbers, or time intervals. The form of the numeric presentation isn't nearly as important as the ability to quantify the measure.

TIP

> If you're having trouble creating a quantifiable measure, you're typically looking at the wrong result. Often you're looking at a result that's too broad. Break this result into smaller components, and you'll find a result that you can measure.

EASY TO UNDERSTAND

One of my clients established an incentive compensation program for all production and administrative personnel. They used several measures to support their overall goal of increased profitability. One of the measures was "return on average capital employed."

I learned that they were using this measure when the vice president of human resources called to ask for my help in communicating the concept. It seems that his initial attempt generated more questions than understanding.

After helping him devise a communiqué, I offered an observation. I told him that there was no way the employees on the shop floor would be able to relate their daily work to the achievement of this measure. Two years later, he told me that my prediction had come true; the employees were viewing the incentive payments as holiday bonuses.

Your employees must be able to understand the measure and relate it to their daily work. If they can't, the measure will not help them improve performance.

WELL BALANCED

We've all heard horror stories that demonstrate the importance of well-balanced goals. I've seen companies set aggressive sales targets without considering the production, service, and financing aspects of their decision. The tragic consequence is that they lose the very customers they fought so hard to get. Why? They failed to honor the promises made in their sales and marketing efforts.

I've seen companies focus so narrowly on reducing the cost of their delivery operations that they angered customers. You can imagine the pain a customer using just-in-time inventory would feel if his deliveries were delayed.

To help you avoid these mistakes, I refer you to a book by David Norton and Robert Kaplan titled *The Balanced Scorecard*. It offers valuable insights into the art of establishing balanced goals. Don't be intimidated by the fact that the approach is designed for company-wide use. The concepts can be used at any level in the organization.

TIP

> Make your employees aware of the danger involved in creating a goal without fully considering the implications of its achievement. It'll help them be more successful. It will also help you avoid dealing with problems that your employees inadvertently created.

EASY TO TRACK

You want to choose measures that facilitate daily, or at least weekly, tracking of results. There is a direct correlation between the frequency with which results are posted and the intensity of your employees' focus. If you only post results once a month, I can assure you that your employees will lose sight of their performance goals. With that thought in mind, let's identify some measures for tracking customer retention.

Customer retention is a worthy goal, but it is not one that lends itself to daily or weekly tracking. There are, however, many aspects of customer retention that do lend themselves to daily measurement:

- Responsiveness to customer inquiries.

- Time involved in satisfactorily resolving customer problems.

- Number of defective parts shipped.

- Billing errors.

- Shipping errors.

Choose measures over which the employee has control. Then post the results daily.

> **CAUTION**
>
> Employees who are held responsible for results outside their control live in constant fear. It's difficult to be productive when you're worried about your future.

If you're wondering why daily tracking is so important, place yourself in the role of the employee. Your boss is posting your results daily. Where are you going to focus your energies? Of course it'll be on the measures being tracked.

The best tracking system is one that allows the employee to monitor his own performance. The value of a self-monitoring system is two-fold. First, it allows the employee to make daily adjustments as necessary to achieve his goals. Second, the employee tends to trust the results more when he can verify them himself.

FREQUENTLY PUBLISHED

You can establish the best possible measures, track them daily, and still not gain the performance improvement you seek. How? The information doesn't get posted. Here's what happened to one of my clients.

This client is a specialty manufacturer dealing in the design and manufacture of custom products for its customers. One measure used in the production department was "production efficiency," the percentage of work completed that day versus the work planned for the day.

Every day someone in the office calculates production efficiency and posts the results on a white board in the plant. The person assigned this task is also responsible for the computer network. One day he experienced problems with the network and forgot to post the results. The next day the same thing happened. The third day he simply forgot to post the measure. (Isn't it amazing how quickly good habits die?) Three months later we observed a decline in the company's profitability. Why? The lack of feedback caused the production employees to lose sight of their goal.

Another equally important reason for posting information daily is that it allows the employee to experience the sense of success more often. Every time we achieve a goal, we experience the feeling of satisfaction. Don't rob your employees of one of the most satisfying aspects of their job. Provide them with frequent feedback.

CURRENT PERFORMANCE

Now it's time to measure current performance. Here's an example.

A construction client's goal is to improve cash flow. A study of the production and billing processes shows that it takes three weeks to invoice the customer after the job is complete. Three weeks is the *current level of performance*.

> **PLAIN ENGLISH**
>
> **Current level of performance** is the result you're getting today. These results are the benchmark against which you and your employees will measure results from improvement initiatives. With each new success you raise the level of current performance and the benchmark used in your measurements.

DESIRED PERFORMANCE

Once you've identified current performance, you have a solid foundation for establishing improvement goals. You'll be asking yourself questions such as, "How much improvement should I target?" or, "How do I know whether my target is aggressive or unrealistic?" The latter question is especially important.

When you establish unrealistic goals, you set your employees, your company, and yourself up for failure. I can't think of anything more devastating than a no-win situation like this. Here are a few ideas on how you can avoid this problem.

First, does the goal promote customer satisfaction? This may seem like a strange question if you're leading an accounts payable function. Yet your actions can affect both the price of the goods your company purchases and the timeliness of the delivery of those goods.

If you cause your vendors to do a lot of paperwork, slow their payments, or are unresponsive to their requests for payment, you limit your company's ability to get further price reductions. You also give vendors reason to place your company farther down on the priority list for shipments. Both of these results affect your company's ability to serve its customers well.

Second, do a cost-benefit analysis. If you're not comfortable doing this analysis on your own, get help from the accounting department. Your goal isn't realistic if the costs of achieving the goal exceed the benefits gained.

Third, are the time frames for accomplishing the goal realistic? Don't misunderstand me; you should choose aggressive time frames. Just make sure they are realistic.

How can you tell whether you've crossed the line? Look at the probability of success. I use 50 percent as my guide. If I have a 50 percent (or better) chance of achieving the goal, I consider it aggressive. If the probability of success is less than 50 percent, it's unrealistic.

TIP

Ask your employees to participate in goal setting. Their familiarity with the work helps you avoid costly mistakes. Their participation in the decision increases their commitment to the goal's success.

Let's assume that your employee is successful and achieves the desired level of performance, then what?

CONTINUOUS IMPROVEMENT

So much is written about *continuous improvement* these days, and rightfully so.

PLAIN ENGLISH

Continuous improvement describes the goal of becoming better at what we do every day of our lives. When applied to organizations, it includes all segments of the company's operations.

The importance of continuous improvement goes well beyond the competitive advantage it affords your company. It allows your employees to enjoy

- Variety in their work.

- Learning opportunities.

- The satisfaction of conquering new challenges.

- The satisfaction of doing valuable work.

- The pride of being associated with a successful company.

Unless you raise the performance bar after each success, you deprive your employees of the opportunity to experience greater job satisfaction. You also rob your company of the financial success it deserves and yourself of the recognition you could earn as a valued leader in your organization.

Some employees may resist your attempts to raise the bar. You may even hear comments like, "Why bother? Once we get there he'll just set a higher goal. It'll never end."

If you don't find ways to improve what you are doing, you will end up doing the same job every day for the rest of your career. You'll learn nothing new, and you won't experience a sense of accomplishment. Your value to the company and yourself will continue to decline and, ultimately, you'll threaten your own financial livelihood.

The language in this statement focuses on what's important to the employee: job satisfaction, employability, and financial success. By providing "selfish" motives, you increase the employee's interest in improving his performance.

THE 30-SECOND RECAP

Performance measures must be

- Quantifiable.

- Easy to understand.

- Well balanced.

- Easy to track.

- Frequently published.

- Specific to the individual employee's work effort.

- Stated in terms of current and desired performance.

- Raised as soon as the desired performance is achieved.

LESSON 3

Encouraging Employee Development

In this lesson, you'll learn about your role as mentor and the performance appraisal's part in fulfilling that role.

BECOMING A MENTOR

Effective performance goals don't assure improved performance. Your employees must possess the skills necessary to convert these goals to reality. In today's fast-paced world, it's difficult for employees to meet deadlines and evaluate their skill development needs. That's why it's essential that you become a *mentor* to all your employees.

PLAIN ENGLISH

A **mentor** is a wise and trusted advisor. Mentors can be found both within and outside your organization. The key is finding someone who possesses skills that you want to develop.

There is more to mentoring than saving time. Mentors provide their protégés with opportunities to view themselves through another's eyes. This is important because it's difficult for us to see our own weaknesses. Often we don't realize that we've developed a bad habit unless someone is kind enough to tell us. Your employees are no different. That's why it's important that they have someone in their lives who cares enough about them to tell them what they need to know about themselves. In the work environment, that's you.

WISDOM

By definition, a mentor is wise. I'm not sure how many of you consider yourselves wise. You are more likely to think of yourself as someone who does a good job.

Your promotion indicates that you have the ability to anticipate what is needed, act based on that information, and produce results well in advance of your peers. Sounds like wisdom to me. Regardless of whether you consider yourself wise, you have a talent you can use to help others.

Your ability to anticipate is the key. You have an intuitive sense for what needs to be done in any situation. Simply apply this skill to your employees' circumstances. How?

Place yourself in the employees' shoes. Use what you know about your employees' strengths, skills, and job requirements to decide what you would do in their circumstances. This analysis provides a map for leading your employees to higher and higher levels of performance and job satisfaction.

TRUST

A mentor must also be trusted. Your employees know when you have their best interests at heart. What does it mean to have their best interest at heart? It means that you

- Want to see them succeed.

- Do everything in your power to help them succeed.

- Want them to have fun on the job.

- Want to see them recognized for their accomplishments.

If your employees sense that the only reason you are encouraging their personal development is to make yourself look good, they will resist your efforts. On the other hand, if they sense that you want them to succeed and that the benefits to you and the company are ancillary, they'll willingly follow your lead.

CAUTION

> Some people have so little confidence in their own abilities that they trust virtually no one. They look for hidden agendas in every opportunity and every word of encouragement you offer. It's rare, but I recently had a client who experienced this phenomenon. Understand the reaction for what it is—a lack of self-confidence.

EVALUATING STRENGTHS

Now that you've demonstrated wisdom and earned your employee's trust, your next goal is to understand the employee's strengths. Here are some questions you need to ask:

- Which tasks does the employee perform well?

- Which tasks cause the employee to struggle?

- What performance measures do you use for each of these tasks?

- What skills will the employee need to improve performance on existing measures?

- Will new measures be required in the future?

- When will the new measures be employed?

- What skills will the employee need to achieve desired results using these new measures?

- Do other employees readily accept this employee's lead?

- Does the employee communicate well?

- Does the employee possess the patience to teach others?

- Does the employee demonstrate the desire to teach?

- Are the employee's motives selfish, selfless, or somewhere in between?

- How would you classify the employee's attitude: optimistic, realistic, or pessimistic?

- Under which conditions does this employee excel: structured, chaotic, or creative?

- Does this employee prefer team or individual efforts?

- How does this employee react to time pressure?

- When faced with new challenges, does the employee jump at the opportunity, hesitate, or run for the hills?

These are representative questions. They form a good foundation on which to build an understanding of your employees' strengths. The answers to these questions will undoubtedly raise other questions that are specific to the individual employee. In the end, you want a clear understanding of the areas in which your employee performs well and what her potential for growth is.

TIP

> Give your employees time to answer these questions. You'll create a new awareness of what's important to their success and help them become more forward thinking.

EXPLORING EMPLOYEE INTERESTS

A friend of mine, a financial planner, shocked me when he told me he might pursue another career. Even though he hadn't been in business very long, he had achieved considerable financial success. When I asked why the change of heart, he responded, "Now that I have proven I can be successful, I have to decide whether this is what I want to do."

This was a real eye-opener for me. I assumed that because he was successful he was enjoying what he was doing. As I examined my career

I realized that I had made similar decisions over the years. Apparently, those weren't the conscious decisions my friend was making.

CAUTION

Don't equate skills with interests. As the previous story demonstrates, to do so is a serious miscalculation; one that may cause an employee to fail because he lacks interest in the work.

The performance appraisal is an excellent tool for discovering your employees' interests. Here are a few questions to help you uncover those interests:

- What is your favorite part of your job? Why?

- What do you like least about the job?

- What would make the least attractive aspect of your work more enjoyable?

- Is there work that you aren't currently doing that appeals to you? Why?

- What skills do you think you'll need to do that work?

- Do your currently possess those skills?

- If not, how would you go about gaining those skills?

The last three questions are designed to measure your employee's level of interest. They'll help you decide whether she's simply dreaming or seriously considering a career change.

If your employee is simply dreaming, make her aware of what she's doing. One of the greatest sources of dissatisfaction in this world is the gap between dreams and reality. Next, get your employee to make a conscious decision. She's either going to pursue the dream or abandon it. The middle ground is fraught with frustration. Help your employees make conscious decisions about their dreams. You'll save yourself, and your employees, a lot of pain.

An employee who has already thought about how he might become involved in other types of work is often bored. There are a variety of ways to deal with boredom. You can

- Add new responsibilities that will challenge the employee.

- Get two employees who are experiencing boredom to change jobs for a while.

- Involve the employee in special projects.

- Have employees examine each other's work to increase efficiency.

- Temporarily trade employees with another leader who shares your leadership style.

Boredom is a thief that quietly robs your employee of her job satisfaction and you of her productivity. The performance appraisal can help you avoid this problem.

TIP

> If restlessness persists, your employee is ready to move on. Don't stand in the way. If possible, help her find what she needs in your organization. It's better to lose a good employee to another department than to a competitor.

MATCHING STRENGTHS AND INTERESTS

As you examine your employee's strengths and interests, compare them to the workload she faces, then answer the following questions:

- Are there mismatches between this employee's workload, skills, and interests?

- Do mismatches exist with other employees as well?

- Will work reassignment cure these mismatches?

- Do the employees have the skills necessary to make reassignment feasible?

- What impact will reassignment have on productivity, both short-term and long-term?

TIP

> Favor interest over skills in assigning work. Over the years I've learned that it is much easier to teach skills than to generate interest. A highly skilled, disinterested worker typically does not perform as well as an interested, less skilled worker.

Before you announce a new and wonderful reassignment plan, meet with the employees who will be affected. These meetings give you a chance to

- Confirm your understanding of their interests.

- Gain insights into concerns they may have.

- Help them overcome any fears they may have.

- Provide insights into how this plan benefits all parties: the employees, the company, and you.

- Change the plan if the design is faulty.

The success of the reassignment plan depends heavily on the employees' belief that they participated in its design.

THE NEED FOR A DEVELOPMENT PLAN

Now that you have a thorough understanding of the employee's strengths and interests and you've identified future skill needs, it's time to help your employee create a *development plan*.

How important is the development plan? You may as well ask how
easy it is to drive to a new location without directions? The development plan is a guide in which you identify

- **The destination**   The skills the employee needs.

- **Available resources**   College courses, public seminars,
  internal training, or experience in other departments or on
  other projects and coaching.

- **Timetables**   Deadlines for acquiring the skills.

Assure that your employees have the skills they need. Help them create a development plan.

CREATING A DEVELOPMENT PLAN

There are two things you can do to increase the effectiveness of a
development plan. First, allow your employee to participate in the
plan's development. Her participation increases the likelihood that
she will act on the plan.

Second, leave the employee to her own devices as much as possible.
This means that if you and your employee have different approaches
for developing a skill and both would work, allow your employee to
choose her method. Why? Her choice will match her learning style,
which, in turn, will speed skill development.

Let's take a look at the steps involved in creating development plans:

1. Ask the employee what skills she thinks she will need in the
   future.

2. Share your thoughts with the employee and ask her opinion.

3. Ask the employee how she would acquire these skills.

4. Encourage the approaches that make sense.

5. Offer other approaches or resources the employee might not have considered.

6. Leave the choice of approaches to the employee, if possible.

7. Agree upon deadlines for each phase of the development plan.

8. Establish rewards for the timely development of each skill.

9. Establish feedback systems that allow the employee to monitor her progress.

10. Use the deadlines as communication triggers for follow-up meetings.

11. Use the information gained in follow-up meetings, good news or bad, to amend the development plan.

TIP

Even though *development plan* is the commonly used terminology in performance appraisals, I believe it implies the "need" to improve. I prefer *future success strategies.* I believe this phrase implies current success.

The approach just outlined simplifies the development plan process, involves the employee in designing the plan, increases the likelihood that she will act on the plan, and provides for periodic follow-up on the employee's progress. It's easy to see why the employee development plan is such an integral part of the performance appraisal process.

THE 30-SECOND RECAP

- Performance improvement requires improvement of skills.

- Your role as mentor is to help your employees improve their skills.

- Employees are more likely to develop skills in areas that interest them.

- Employees are more successful when they participate in the creation of their own development plan.

LESSON 4

Striving for Employee Satisfaction

In this lesson, you'll learn about the benefits of employee satisfaction, factors that influence satisfaction, and the performance appraisal's role in making work enjoyable.

THE BENEFITS OF HAVING HAPPY EMPLOYEES

In their book *Raving Fans,* Ken Blanchard and Sheldon Bowles offer numerous examples of how ecstatic employees take customer service to stratospheric levels. In addition to being great ambassadors for your company, happy employees are

- More likely to stay with the company.

- Are absent fewer days than unhappy employees.

- File fewer grievances.

- Complete their work more quickly.

- Produce higher-quality work.

- Find ways to improve their effectiveness.

- Share their enthusiasm with colleagues.

To help us understand the enormity of these benefits, let's look at each more closely.

RETENTION

Today's hottest business topic is employee retention. Globally, companies are experiencing high rates of growth coupled with low unemployment. Is it any wonder that leaders are focused on ways to retain their employees?

What are the ramifications of losing an employee? What does it cost financially? Psychologically? The initial cost comes in the form of lost productivity. When you lose a team member, your options are to

- Ask the remaining employees to pick up additional work.

- *Outsource* some of the work to a temporary help agency.

- Reevaluate the workload of the entire team and determine what, if any, work can be eliminated or postponed.

PLAIN ENGLISH

Outsource is a term that describes the company's decision to use outside services rather than have employees perform the tasks. Companies outsource tasks such as payroll and training.

If you choose the first option, you run the risk of creating more unhappy employees and more retention problems. Even if you are a strong leader and unconcerned about further losses, you face heavy costs in the form of

- Additional overtime.

- Lower productivity due to fatigue.

- Higher absenteeism caused by illness associated with fatigue.

- Rework caused by errors resulting from fatigue.

- Missed deadlines.

- Lost momentum on new initiatives.

As you can see, it doesn't take long for the costs to mount.

TIP

If you choose to spread the work among your remaining employees, allow them to participate in the decisions about how work should be reallocated. This approach minimizes their dissatisfaction with the increasing workload.

Outsourcing brings its own set of costs. If you choose to use a temporary help agency

1. You or someone in your department has to spend time finding an agency with the right talent pool.

2. Someone has to take time to train the person.

3. Higher levels of supervision are required because the work is unfamiliar to the person.

4. Even with additional supervision, errors are going to occur more frequently, which increases the amount of rework and the total amount of work to be accomplished.

5. The additional demands on you and your team make it difficult to plan far enough ahead to keep the temporary person productive throughout the day.

By the way, items two through four have to be repeated when you finally hire a permanent replacement.

The third option, reevaluating the work, can be a benefit. The old adage, "Necessity is the mother of invention," is true. The loss of a team member often spawns some very creative ideas for accomplishing the work more quickly. How? By identifying redundant or trivial tasks that can be eliminated. The problem is that your team is trying to create these efficiencies when they are already burdened with extra work. The best time for this activity is *before* you lose an employee.

TIP

Wait until you're fully staffed and in the midst of your slow season (most businesses have one) to embark on a reevaluation of your team's work.

ABSENTEEISM

Employee absences are inevitable, and the number of absences is increasing. The "sandwich" generation, those people in their 50s and 60s today, find themselves caring for three generations: themselves, their children, and their parents.

Combine these additional care requirements with the plethora of dual wage-earner families and you have escalating absenteeism. Add the occasional car breakdown, ice or snowstorm, and parent-teacher conference, and you can see that employee absences are indeed inevitable.

What impact does an absence have? First, you've got to drop what you're doing to evaluate what needs to be done that day. Then you have to disrupt someone else's (maybe several other people's) schedule, explain what needs to be done, make yourself available to answer their inevitable questions, then follow up frequently to make sure that deadlines are met.

You are easily facing losses of one to two hours for each person involved. That's a loss in productivity of 15 percent or more, and we haven't even discussed the costs associated with overtime, lost momentum on new initiatives, or the wear and tear on those who are handling the additional workload.

Employees who enjoy their work find ways to minimize their absences. They realize the burden it places on their teammates and they do everything in their power to avoid hurting the team.

Conversely, employees who are unhappy look for reasons not to come to work. I recently completed work with a client who was spending $84,000 a year for overtime and another $39,000 for temporary help to cover employee absences. Virtually all of the $123,000 could be traced to absences associated with employee dissatisfaction. That's a hefty price tag.

GRIEVANCES

If you work in a union environment, you know that the *grievance* process is expensive. You spend time researching your position, creating a defense, involving the legal department or an outside attorney, and testifying at the proceeding. All these activities take you away from your primary responsibilities.

> **PLAIN ENGLISH**
>
> A **grievance** is a formal complaint filed by a union employee against the employer, which is supported by the union. Some nonunion companies have similar procedures for dealing with employee complaints.

Even if you win, you face the possibility of retribution from the employee and, possibly, his co-workers as well. Usually acts of retribution are crafted to create problems without violating the terms of the contract. I don't need to calculate these costs for you. You know they're huge.

Happy employees file grievances only when someone in management violates the contract. Unhappy employees look for reasons to file grievances. They really don't care whether their claim is ultimately deemed frivolous. They have accomplished their goal: creating problems for you.

> **TIP**
>
> If you have an employee who is frequently filing grievances, ask him to participate in making decisions. It's difficult to complain about a decision that you helped make.

PRODUCTIVITY AND QUALITY

You need to look no further than your own performance to evaluate the impact happiness has on productivity and quality. Think of a task that you don't enjoy. Are you happy when you're doing the work? Since the work isn't pleasant, do you tend to postpone it? When you finally get around to tackling the job, are you bumping up against the deadline? Does the delay cause you to take shortcuts to meet the deadline? Have these shortcuts resulted in errors? Did the errors result in your having to redo the work? This picture is getting really ugly, isn't it?

Now let's look at a task you enjoy. This work gets priority status because you enjoy it. Deadlines aren't a problem; you usually complete the work early. You seldom make errors, so the need for rework is virtually eliminated. This simple comparison makes it easy to see how important employee satisfaction is to productivity and quality.

INCREASING EFFECTIVENESS

Unhappy employees will do a reliable job, if you're lucky. At best, they'll do what is asked of them. Generally they'll do enough to retain their jobs, nothing more. Today's competitive environment requires a commitment to continuous improvement from every employee. You're not going to get that commitment from an unhappy employee.

Conversely, people who enjoy their work typically look forward to new opportunities. They look for ways to accomplish their work more quickly so that they can learn and grow. They are committed to continuous improvement.

TIP

> The effectiveness of your team depends heavily on your ability to assure each employee's satisfaction with his or her job.

ENTHUSIASM

Happiness and unhappiness share a common quality: They are both contagious. Think of someone, a friend or co-worker, who is always complaining. How do you feel when you're with that person? Does he sap your energy? Does life seem a little less worthwhile? Worse yet, does he destroy your good moods?

Now contrast the feelings you have when you're with an upbeat person. Do you laugh more often? What happens to your energy level? It soars! Do you experience a renewed zest for living? You bet you do.

Your employee's satisfaction with the job is going to determine his impact on co-workers, customers, vendors, and you.

How expensive is the lack of enthusiasm? What's the value of a customer? How important is the vendor to your ability to honor commitments to your customers? What's the cost when an unhappy employee drives away happy employees? What's it worth to you to work with people who are upbeat and committed to success?

Now that you've seen how valuable employee satisfaction is, let's see what it takes to ensure their happiness.

WHAT MAKES EMPLOYEES HAPPY?

All right, let's be honest. How many of you think money makes employees happy? It's the one thing that everyone desires. Even billionaires like Bill Gates, Warren Buffett, and Michael Dell want more money. Not because they have unsatisfied lifestyle needs; they can afford any creature comfort they desire. Their desire is for greater success. Money is just the way they keep score.

For those of us who may not be able to dream quite that big, money holds the promise of a more comfortable lifestyle. Is it logical, then, to conclude that more money will make an employee happy? It may be logical, but it isn't factual. I know from personal experience that having more money doesn't lead to greater happiness.

Years ago, I was on the verge of quitting when the boss offered me more money. I thought the money would compensate for the less desirable aspects of the job. It didn't. Three months later I hated the job even more and felt guilty for having thoughts of leaving. The allure of money is great and it often clouds our judgment. Don't delude yourself into thinking that you can buy your employees' happiness with money.

What role should money play in an employee's happiness? As mentioned earlier, its greatest value is as a means of keeping score, a reward for success. Tie your employees' compensation to their performance, give them the ability to track their own progress, then reward them financially for achieving their goals. That's how you use money to promote employee satisfaction.

VARIETY

I recently worked with a group of data entry personnel to improve morale. Their work is very repetitive and *boring*, yet it is vital to the company's operation. One of the things we did was allow the employees to bring headsets to work so that they could listen to their favorite radio station or play CDs. We saw an immediate increase in productivity and drop in the absentee rate. Why? Variety was added to their daily routine.

You can accomplish similar results by periodically shifting work between employees, involving them in new projects, or possibly trading employees with another department for short periods of time. The method you choose isn't as important as assuring variety. After all, boredom is the bane of productivity.

TIP

> Over the years I've found that nonmonetary aspects of the job—things like variety, learning, growth, and recognition—are more important to most employees than the money.

GROWTH OPPORTUNITIES

People don't enjoy the status quo. If you doubt that, think about one of the important achievements in your life. How long was it before you began to think about your next goal? The satisfaction that comes from goal achievement is fleeting. You enjoy it only for a few days or weeks, then you look for the next challenge to conquer.

I'm sure that some of you are thinking, "But that isn't true of all my employees. There are some who are very content doing the same job day in, day out." I believe you.

People who don't aspire to leadership roles are often very happy in their support roles. That doesn't mean they aren't interested in growth, it simply means they aren't interested in moving up the organization chart.

There is another type of growth that's available even in today's *flatter organizations*. That's growth within the job. This type of growth allows the employee to learn new skills and take on new responsibilities in his present position. Personal growth is both emotionally satisfying and financially rewarding.

PLAIN ENGLISH

Flatter organizations is a phrase used to describe businesses that have reduced the number of layers of management. In the 1960s and '70s many companies had six or more layers of management. Today that number is four or less.

It's emotionally satisfying because the employee enjoys feeling that he is becoming better every day. It's financially rewarding because he is making himself more valuable to the company. Help your employees understand the importance of growth, not just for the company, but for themselves. You'll dramatically increase their enjoyment of the work.

LEARNING

If you look at *Fortune* magazine's list of the "100 Best Companies to Work For," you'll find that all these companies invest heavily in training. Why? Their leaders recognize that employees

- Must improve their skills for the company to thrive.

- Feel good about themselves when they learn.

- Appreciate, respect, and readily follow leaders who regularly invest in their personal growth.

Your company doesn't need the training budget of a Fortune 500 company to provide learning. In fact, you don't have to have a training budget at all. That may sound like heresy from someone who offers training as part of his consulting work, but the reality is that learning comes in many forms. You can

- Involve employees in projects requiring new skills.

- Use cross training to teach new skills.

- Have one of your best performers demonstrate the techniques that make him successful.

- Use book reviews to promote the learning of new skills.

The opportunities are limitless.

TIP

> Don't feel compelled to come up with these ideas on your own. Ask your employees what they would like to learn.

PARTICIPATION

Are you the master of your own destiny? Do you want to be? Of course you do. Ever since the age of two you've been asserting your independence. That's why you become irritated when your boss tells you what to do, when to do it, and how it should be done. Your employees feel the same way. That's why it's important to involve them in decisions regarding their work.

Ask your employees to participate in establishing performance measures, deadlines, goals, and priorities. Allow them to choose their own approaches to the work. Give them the opportunity to build their own development plans. They'll enjoy the job much more knowing that they participated in making these decisions.

RECOGNITION

Is there any greater reward than public recognition? Who among us hasn't dreamed of having our name in lights? Yet most of us view the odds to be roughly the same as winning the lottery.

CAUTION

> Many people lose their desire to improve simply because their results aren't recognized.

It doesn't have to be that way for your employees. You control the spotlight. Shine it on their successes. Let them know that you are aware they're doing a wonderful job.

One of the more common mistakes leaders make is recognizing only top performers. There are employees who do a marvelous job yet get little, if any, recognition for their efforts. Here's how one of my clients addressed that issue. Every day he would list both the top performers and those who had achieved new personal bests. I love this concept. The people, who would never be able to achieve the title "Best," still have an opportunity to be recognized for their accomplishments.

You can add a team dimension to this recognition system by celebrating days when the team sets a record for new personal bests. The celebration can be as simple as ordering pizza or bringing in ice cream.

I've let my team off an hour early on Friday afternoon when they have had an incredibly successful week. The form of recognition isn't as important as the recognition itself. Don't overlook this opportunity to make your employees' jobs more satisfying.

SECURITY

Is security a thing of the past? Many employees fear that it is. The merger and acquisition activities of the past decade seem to indicate that they're right—that is if you view security as continued employment with the same company.

There is another form of security that you can offer your employees that is just as valuable. The key is to help them understand the "new" definition of security.

The only real security is ability—specifically, the ability to produce results. If employees understand this and they use the performance appraisal to guide their success, they'll contribute significantly to their future employability. That's important, considering the likelihood of falling victim to a merger or acquisition.

Will increased employability remove the pain and fear associated with a job loss? Absolutely not! It can, however, minimize the time it takes to find comparable employment.

During the performance appraisal process, emphasize that hitting performance targets and development plan goals is as important to their future employability as it is to the company's success.

EMPLOYEE DIFFERENCES

Life would be simple if all employees valued all the job satisfaction factors equally. Alas, it is not to be. Some employees are driven by money. Others value recognition above the other factors. To some, security is the top priority.

TIP

> Differences between employees are part of the variety of your job. Don't bemoan them. Your job would be very boring without them.

One of the advantages of performance appraisals is that they enable you to explore each employee's wants and needs. One approach is to simply ask your employees to rank each of the satisfaction factors in order of importance.

A less direct approach is to ask the employee how each factor influences his job satisfaction. It'll be easy to tell which factors are important by the sheer volume of ideas they express. The factors that elicit no ideas aren't important; those that generate five ideas in 15 seconds are.

THE 30-SECOND RECAP

Employee satisfaction is a key element of performance improvement. Factors that influence employee satisfaction are

- Variety.
- Growth.
- Learning.
- Participation.
- Recognition.
- Security.

LESSON 5
Compensating Employees

In this lesson, you'll learn about the connection between compensation, performance, and performance appraisal.

A COMMON OCCURRENCE

It's time for your performance appraisal and salary review. As you reflect on the past year, you realize that

- You haven't missed any work.

- The only deadline you missed was caused by another department's failure to provide the information you needed.

- Your boss has not criticized your performance; in fact, you have received a few compliments during the year.

- The few errors you made did not result in major rework; besides, the boss didn't seem concerned about them.

- You get along well with your co-workers.

- You have good working relationships with colleagues in other departments.

- You pitched in and helped your boss with a couple of projects when asked.

Overall, you're proud of your performance and you think that your raise is going to be on the upper end of the scale.

Your boss calls you into her office, hands you a copy of the appraisal, and gives you a few minutes to read it. You're delighted to see that her appraisal is closely aligned with your thoughts. Then you see it, a comment at the bottom of the last page. It says that you don't demonstrate initiative. It goes on to say that you have leadership potential, but you aren't assuming the role of a leader.

This is the first time you've heard these comments. You had no idea the boss saw leadership qualities in you. You certainly have never viewed yourself that way. You're flattered that someone would consider you a leader, then you realize that this comment is a criticism of your performance. You wonder whether it's going to affect your raise.

Your question is answered almost before its formed. The boss says that your raise will be the standard raise for someone at your level in the organization. She goes on to say that if you had taken the initiative to assume a leadership role that your increase would have been much higher. She hopes that you will take that initiative in the coming year.

How do you feel? Do you think you've been treated fairly? Would you have assumed the leadership role had you known it was expected of you? Do the compliments you received during the course of the year mean anything to you now? Of course not!

At this point, you feel betrayed. You cannot believe that your boss evaluated you on an expectation she hadn't communicated. You also find it hard to believe that you're being penalized for missing a goal you didn't know existed. Yet the penalty is there in the form of a lower raise.

At this point, what's your attitude toward the coming year? Are you excited about your prospects or are you wondering how you'll be blindsided next year? Do you have an interest in your boss's success? Are you considering other employment?

Your satisfaction with the job is rapidly approaching zero. I don't care how well your boss used the employee satisfaction factors listed in Lesson 4, "Striving for Employee Satisfaction"; everything she gained from those efforts just evaporated.

TIP

It's easy to anticipate an employee's reaction to any situation: Simply put yourself in her place. There's a commonality to our humanity that allows us to use our experiences to anticipate the reaction of others.

AVOIDING PROBLEMS

Besides communicating more effectively, what can you do to avoid these problems? One solution is to chronologically separate performance appraisals from salary reviews. I prefer a six-month interval between the two. Here's why.

The performance appraisal gives me an opportunity to think about my employees, how they can improve, and what I expect from them. During the performance appraisal meeting the employee and I discuss future levels of performance and reach an agreement on what that performance should be. We also discuss compensation for each level of performance. Then I monitor his performance for six months.

I use a six-month time frame because it allows me to evaluate behavioral changes. Most employees can change their behavior for a month or two, long enough to get a raise, then they revert to old habits. If they change their behaviors for six months, they've formed new habits. When the new behaviors produce the desired results, the salary review becomes a cause for celebration.

Even when the employee isn't completely successful, the salary review is easier for both parties. Both of you know what the goals are. Both of you agreed what the salary increase will be for each level of performance. As long as the tracking system allows the two of you to monitor the employee's progress, there should be no disagreement over the amount of the increase.

CAUTION

> Here's another reason to be specific in the performance
> measures you use: Lack of clarity in the results to be
> measured invites conflict.

THE VALUE PROPOSITION

Compensation is a reward for producing results. The value of the
result must exceed the amount of the reward, or the company loses
money. This is a simple concept, right? Then how is it that so many
companies have people on their payrolls who are "overpaid"?

Here are some of reasons why compensation and results get out of
synch. Leaders

- Don't quantify the value of results.

- Fail to raise expectations.

- Place too much emphasis on past performance.

- Don't require employees to think in terms of value.

Let's look at each of these in more detail.

QUANTIFYING VALUE

Value and improvement don't always go hand in hand. Remember the
printing company example in Lesson 1, "The Goals of Performance
Appraisal"? My friend explained that the difference between a good
print job and a great print job is imperceptible to most customers. For
that reason, most customers won't pay for the extra quality. The same
can be true for other types of improvement.

Here's another example. The collection department's responsibility is
to assure that customers pay on time. Let's assume that, on average,
customers are taking 33 days to pay their invoices. The company's
terms are "Net 30," which means that the invoice is due 30 days after
the invoice date. In essence, customers are paying three days late.

Let's say that you want the collection department to bring the average collection period down from 33 days to 31 days. What questions do you need to ask to determine whether that improvement has value? Consider these:

1. How much will we collect by reducing the collection period by two days?

2. How will that money be used?

3. If it's used to repay loans, how much will we save on interest charges?

4. If the additional cash is used to invest in the company's growth, what kind of return can we expect?

5. Will we need more collectors to accomplish this goal? If not, will there be any overtime associated with the extra effort?

6. What's the likelihood that we'll antagonize our customers by calling so quickly after the due date on the invoice?

7. How much will it cost us if we lose a customer because of the heightened collection efforts?

8. How much lost business does it take to overcome the benefits of a shorter collection period?

TIP

> Whenever you are evaluating a performance measure for possible improvement, ask yourself these two value questions. What will it cost to achieve this higher level of performance? How much profit or savings will the improvement generate?

I realize that many of you are not accustomed to converting performance measures into dollars and cents. If you struggle with these "value" questions, go to your company's controller and ask for help.

One of the accounting department's functions is to help operating managers understand the financial impact of their decisions.

CAUTION

> Improvement ideas can be exciting. Excitement can cause you to overlook the value questions. Whenever you feel yourself becoming enamoured with an idea, take a deep breath and ask the value questions. You'll save yourself at lot of headaches.

FAILING TO RAISE EXPECTATIONS

Often this mistake is made with your best performers. These people make your life so easy that you hate to rock the boat by suggesting they do more. Truthfully, you do them a disservice by failing to raise expectations. You rob them of opportunities for variety, growth, learning, and greater success. Often you create compensation problems as well. Here's how.

Even good performers reach performance plateaus, stages at which they find it difficult to see improvement opportunities. Unless you established performance goals during the last appraisal, you may not realize that your employee has hit a plateau. She still contributes significantly to the team's success, so you give her a substantial raise.

Again, you resist raising expectations because "she's doing such a fine job." The second year, performance hasn't increased, but it's still solid. You grant another substantial increase. You can see where this is headed. Without your help, expectations aren't raised, and the employee becomes a mediocre performer when measured against the salary she's getting. That's a problem you can avoid: Raise expectations every year.

EMPHASIZING PAST PERFORMANCE

Loyalty is a wonderful quality, until you allow it to cloud your judgment. I see this happen all too often. A leader knows an employee's performance is declining, but finds it difficult to address the issue because the employee contributed so much in earlier years. The leader compounds the problem by giving the employee an annual raise. Now there's a losing proposition: declining productivity and increasing costs.

Unfortunately, I've seen this practice continued for years, with both the leader and the employee becoming increasingly disenchanted with their relationship. The solution is obvious. First, don't give raises unless performance has improved. Second, tell your employee about performance problems as soon as you recognize them. That's the correct way to demonstrate loyalty.

TIP

Don't postpone the handling of problems. I've never seen them get better on their own.

HELPING EMPLOYEES UNDERSTAND VALUE

It's not enough that you understand how to value a performance improvement opportunity. You must teach your employees to do the same.

Earlier I discussed the fact that you were promoted to help others develop the skills that make you so successful. Teaching your employees to understand the value of performance improvement is one of those skills.

If you take the time to teach your employees how to quantify value, you accomplish two goals. First you enable them to work with greater autonomy, which means that you'll spend less time supervising and more time planning the future. Second, you'll enable your employees to create greater value with less effort. That'll make both of you look good.

Conversely, your failure to teach employees how to quantify value is an invitation for them to act on improvement ideas without understanding the idea's full impact. That's a risk neither of your careers can afford.

You can see how easy it is for compensation and performance to get out of synch. You also have a better understanding of the link between value and compensation. Now let's examine the two most common forms of compensation, base pay and incentive pay.

BASE PAY

Since most leaders have little influence over the benefit component of base compensation, we are going to limit our discussion to salary and salary increases.

Most employees, other than salespeople, are paid a base salary or an hourly rate. Many of these employees are satisfied with annual increases that allow them to keep pace with inflation. In other words, they want an increase that's large enough that they don't have to reduce their lifestyle. Employees first became aware of the connection between salary and inflation in the late 60s and early 70s when union leaders pushed for cost-of-living increases.

A problem occurs when employees focus on inflationary increases. They limit their success. Their "decision" to be satisfied with a minimal increase causes them to "decide" on the minimum level of performance necessary to get that increase. Don't let your employees fall into this trap. Help them realize their full potential from both a performance and a compensation standpoint.

LARGE VS. SMALL ORGANIZATIONS

In *large organizations,* your ability to grant raises is limited. Usually salary ranges are associated with job categories. Each category also has a range of allowable base pay increases.

> **PLAIN ENGLISH**
>
> My definition of a **large organization** is one that has more than 200 employees.

If you have an employee whom you want to reward with a larger increase, you'll probably need to get approval from above. You can improve your odds for getting the increase by demonstrating the value of your employee's performance. Your best employees earn the right to higher compensation. When you fail them, you invite their departure.

Smaller organizations face a different set of problems. Often formal pay structures don't exist. Raises are granted more on the employee's ability to negotiate than on the merits of his performance. One of the complaints I hear most often in smaller organizations is inequity. The employees' displeasure stems from

- A lack of performance measures.

- The leader's fondness for one employee over another.

- The dependence of the amount of the increase on the employee's negotiating skills.

Performance appraisals provide the means to increase fairness in compensation decisions.

INCENTIVE COMPENSATION

The form that incentive compensation takes is limited only by your imagination. Several factors are critical to the success of an incentive compensation program. They are

- A clearly defined, well-communicated goal.

- A realistic possibility of success.

- Knowledge of the value to be created by achieving the goal.

- An idea of the percentage of value you wish to share with your employee.

- A feedback system that prevents unpleasant surprises.

- An agreement as to how the incentive will be calculated and when it will be paid.

If your incentive program contains these critical elements, you have an excellent chance of achieving the goal and retaining a valuable employee.

TIP

> I advise clients that once they've outlined the program, they need to switch hats. Take off the leader's hat and put on the employee's hat. Now look for ways to abuse the system.

Unfortunately, I've seen leaders abandon incentive programs because they couldn't prevent abuse. Don't forgo the advantages of an incentive program simply because one or two people may abuse it. You're much better off removing the abusing employees than abandoning a worthwhile incentive pay program.

THE 30-SECOND RECAP

- Do not combine performance appraisals and salary reviews.

- Not all performance improvements are valuable.

- Learn to quantify the value of performance improvements.

- Teach your employees how to calculate the value of performance improvements.

- Tie compensation to the value produced.

LESSON 6
Improving Communication

In this lesson, you'll learn about the importance of communication skills to your employee's performance. You'll also learn about the role of communication in your success as a leader.

THE IMPACT OF POOR COMMUNICATION

How does the pace of today's world impact communication? Think about your e-mail. Have you gotten into the habit of writing partial sentences? In your haste, do you sometimes forget the salutation?

In communications with employees, how often do you feel like saying, "Just do it this way"? How often do you actually use that approach?

Time pressures cause us to place greater emphasis on "doing" than on "communicating." Unless we're working we feel that we're falling farther behind. Our employees feel the same way. Yet if I were to ask you and your employees to identify the single greatest cause of workplace problems, your answer most likely would be poor communication, and you'd be right.

TIP

When you are tempted to use shortcuts in your communiqués, ask yourself how long, it will take the person to redo the job if it's done incorrectly. Then ask yourself how long it will take you to give the proper instructions.

The vast majority of rework performed is the result of poor communication. It's not that employees' skills are inadequate, it's that they don't understand what's being asked of them. Rework is a drain on productivity. In a world where speed is a competitive advantage, there is no time for rework.

So far I've focused on your communications with your employees. It is equally important for your employees to communicate well with you, their teammates, and co-workers in other departments. Every employee has the potential to create rework through poor communication. It's your job to help them improve their skills. The performance appraisal can help. To see how, let's examine the impact that communication has on our lives.

The dynamics of personal interaction are affected by the way we communicate. We can ingratiate ourselves with others and in doing so garner cooperation whenever we need it.

We also have the ability to offend others. How much cooperation do you give people who've offended you? Do you do just enough to keep yourself out of trouble? That's a natural reaction, but it certainly doesn't promote a constructive work environment.

We could spend time discussing how poor communication creates frustration, adds stress, promotes conflict (sometimes to the point of violence), but you already know these things. Let's focus on how the performance appraisal can help your employees become better communicators.

TIP

Model the type of communication that you want your employees to use. Your actions are more powerful communicators than your words.

THE KEYS TO EFFECTIVE COMMUNICATION

Here are some of the things that you should be observing in order to improve your employees' communication skills:

- Completeness of their communications.

- Their ability to listen while communicating.

- Respect for others.

- Style: dictatorial, cooperative, submissive, or parental.

- The impact their mood has on their communications.

- The tone of the communiqué.

Let's explore each of these in more detail.

COMPLETE COMMUNIQUÉS

Does the employee regularly communicate all that the listener needs to know? If not, what types of information does the employee fail to communicate? The answer to the latter question will provide powerful insights into your employee's motivation.

Usually incomplete communications are quite innocent. The speaker simply credits the listener with more knowledge than he has. The absence of malice doesn't alter the fact that this assumption has the potential to create a lot of problems.

Lost productivity is a problem we've already discussed. Another problem is the effect this error has on the relationship between the two parties. The listener may feel betrayed, set up for failure, even though there was no such intent.

This attitude is contagious. The listener tells other members of the team of the betrayal and warns them to be alert so that it doesn't happen to them. The effect on morale is devastating. Amazing, isn't it? A nasty situation like this can arise from an innocent mistake.

Make your employees aware of the disastrous effect incomplete communiqués have on themselves and their co-workers.

CAUTION

> A person who is trying to overcome the habit of incomplete communication will often go overboard and provide too much detail. The risk here is that the listener will feel that his intelligence is being insulted. Help your employees strike a balance between too much and too little detail.

LISTENING

How often have we heard that a good communicator is also a good listener? The questions and comments we get in response to our communiqués are the keys to effective communication. That's the good news. The bad news is that listeners offer us a wide array of feedback other than questions and comments.

Listeners who lack confidence don't often ask questions. They are afraid of appearing stupid. Instead, they'll restate what you said. Paraphrasing is their technique for eliciting more information. If the restatement is broad, they're struggling with the whole concept. You need to start over. Explain the goal and each step that you envision in accomplishing that goal.

If the restatement is specific to one area of your communiqué, then you need to elaborate only on that area. Attempts to review the whole concept will be viewed as condescending and reinforce the listener's feelings of inadequacy.

As strange as it may seem, overly confident listeners also don't ask questions. Their problem is that they don't think about the approach they'll use. They simply act. If you know that your listener has this tendency, make your communiqué more detailed than you might normally. You cannot rely on this listener's feedback to assure effective communication, so don't.

TIP

> If an employee isn't asking questions and you're not
> sure whether he lacks confidence or is overly confident,
> try to recall the employee's actions toward similar types
> of activities. His past performance will help you identify
> his current mindset.

One of the most unusual situations I encountered as a leader involved one of my best employees. Her performance was solid and she was happy to do anything asked of her, but whenever I gave her a new project I'd have to repeat the entire instructions at least twice. It was maddening. We discussed this problem in earlier performance appraisals, but unfortunately neither of us could pinpoint the source of the problem.

Since this was the only individual on the team who posed this problem, I kept wondering what I was doing differently in my communications with her. One day while we were discussing a new project, I noticed that she was looking at the outline I'd provided. She didn't seem to be listening to what I was saying. From the look on her face it appeared that she was forming questions that she wanted to ask. That's when I realized what was happening.

Her mind was so busy developing questions that she didn't have the ability to listen effectively. That's why I had to repeat everything to her twice. I stopped my instructions and shared this insight with her. She quickly confirmed what I'd surmised. At that point we both knew what the problem was. Here's the solution we created.

I promised to allow her as much time as she needed to ask any questions she might have. In return she promised to focus her attention on my instructions as I provided them. It worked beautifully. We were both relieved of frustration that had plagued us for a couple of years.

My point in relating this story is that not all feedback is verbal. Pay attention to facial expressions, hesitation in the voice, and posture to help you evaluate the clarity of your message. Then teach your employees these skills.

RESPECT

We have a right to be respected until we fail to respect others. Are your employees respectful of the feelings of others? Do their communications

- Indicate a respect for the other person's abilities?

- Credit others with the ability to learn quickly?

- Indicate an interest in the other person's welfare?

- Recognize that the ideas of others have value?

- Attempt to elevate others or tear them down?

These questions should be asked and answered in the performance appraisal.

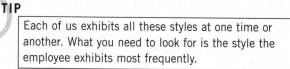

CAUTION

If you have an employee who enjoys kidding others, make sure that you let him know when his kidding becomes disrespectful of his co-workers.

STYLE

People exhibit four styles of communication:

- Dictatorial

- Cooperative

- Submissive

- Parental

TIP

Each of us exhibits all these styles at one time or another. What you need to look for is the style the employee exhibits most frequently.

Dictators dominate conversations and demand that their ideas be accepted. Dictators tend to irritate, frustrate, and incite to riot those with whom they work. If your employee exhibits this style, take action immediately. This person's development plan should have persuasion skills as the top priority. It's your job to teach your employees that communications that influence are more powerful than those that control.

Employees who demonstrate a natural instinct for cooperative communication are golden. Theirs are the voices of sanity in times of disagreement. They are the ones who find the common ground, gain agreement, and move the team forward. This is the style that you want to see in all your employees.

The submissive style is at the opposite end of the spectrum from the dictatorial style. Employees who prefer this style often suffer silently, allowing others to impose their will on them. On the top of their development plans should be assertiveness training. Get them the help they need to develop a cooperative style. Their current style robs them of job satisfaction and deprives you of ideas that might enhance your team's success.

Most of us hate the parental style almost as much as we do the dictatorial. Parents tell us what to do. This is fine when we're small children and don't have a lot of experience from which to draw. It's condescending and downright irritating when we're adults. If you see an employee exhibiting this style, explain to him what he is doing and the reaction others have to this style.

Mood

A person who is normally upbeat and supportive might, on a bad day, become abrupt, insensitive, and sometimes downright belligerent in his communication. If you see this happening, simply say, "It appears that you're having a rough day. We all do from time to time. I'm not asking you to put on a false face, but do you think it's right to take your frustration out on your teammates?" Usually this is enough to get the person to ease up on his co-workers. It may even help change the troubled employee's mood.

People who are regularly in a bad mood exhibit the abruptness, insensitivity, and belligerence mentioned above; they also discourage communication. The absence of communication will inevitably lead to errors, missed deadlines, and a diminution of team effectiveness.

Foul moods are also contagious. If you don't take action, you'll see your absentee rates rise, a can-do attitude replaced with a can't-do attitude, and a rapid decline in productivity. You also risk the loss of your best performers.

Why? Top performers gain energy for others who share their upbeat outlook on life. It's important to their success. They're not going to get that from someone who is riding an emotional roller coaster.

Identifying the cause of mood swings is generally beyond the expertise of most leaders. Your responsibilities are

1. To make the employee aware of the problem.

2. To suggest counseling.

3. If your company employs resources for this purpose, make the employee aware of these resources.

4. To tell the employee that this behavior will not be acceptable in the future.

5. To tell the employee that you are always available should she want a friendly ear.

6. To do nothing more than listen if the employee takes advantage of the offer in number 5.

7. To make mood improvement a focal point in performance appraisals.

> **TIP**
>
> If the employee demonstrates a pattern of mood swings, don't wait until the next performance appraisal to address the problem. Take action immediately. Tolerating this behavior sends a message that it is acceptable.

TONE

Is the tone of your employees' communication upbeat and encouraging, factual and unemotional, or critical and discouraging? Obviously, you prefer the tone to be upbeat and encouraging. You can tolerate factual and unemotional. The critical and discouraging part must change.

People who consistently criticize others are often burdened by their own feelings of inadequacy. Tearing others down is, in their minds, a way of making themselves look better. This is another situation in which counseling may be needed. I suggest using the same approach outlined for frequent mood swings.

Transforming employees who prefer the factual, unemotional tone into encouragers isn't difficult, but may take a little time. First, model the behavior you would like to see them adopt. Second, ask the employees the following questions:

- How do you feel when someone encourages you?

- Do you enjoy working with people who encourage you?

- Are you more likely to help someone who is encouraging?

- Is that how you would like others to view you?

The key is to get your employee to see how he reacts emotionally to someone who is encouraging. That makes it easy for him to understand how others react to this style. This approach, getting people to examine their own reactions, is one of the most powerful I've ever employed.

TIP

The technique of asking questions that help others understand their emotional reactions is one that will serve your employees well in their communications with others. Add the acquisition of this skill to their development plans.

Now that I've identified the aspects of communication that should be evaluated in performance appraisals, let's see how performance appraisals improve communication with employees.

THE ROLE OF COMMUNICATION IN PERFORMANCE APPRAISALS

The performance appraisal is your safety net in the world of communication. It allows you to recover when you drop the ball by failing to

- Recognize your employees' accomplishments.

- Correct recurring errors.

- Communicate expectations.

- Indicate your interest in their success.

- Provide guidance on their personal development.

The performance appraisal is a time to rectify these failings. Please don't misinterpret that statement. I am not suggesting that you wait until the performance appraisal to communicate with your employees. Performance appraisals are no substitute for the daily communications your employees need. You must communicate new expectations, provide feedback on performance, recognize success, and help them deal with their problems each and every day. Once every six months is not enough.

Having said that, I realize that even the best leaders are going to drop the communication ball from time to time. There will be some aspect of performance that should have been communicated, but wasn't. Performance appraisals give you the opportunity to correct this oversight.

In Lesson 1, "The Goals of Performance Appraisal," we discussed communication triggers. These are valuable tools, especially for those of you who have not developed the habit of communicating on a regular basis. Here are a few suggestions for their use:

1. Use multiple triggers.

2. List the triggers on your calendar.

3. Follow up religiously on all *communication triggers*.

PLAIN ENGLISH

Communication triggers are dates, performance goals or other quantifiable measures that, when reached, require you to communicate with your employees.

Over the years, I've witnessed a lot of pain and heartache caused by the failure to use multiple triggers, specifically the failure to combine performance goals and deadlines. I can assure you that if left unstated, your deadline and your employee's deadline will be completely different.

Here's an example of how to combine performance goals and deadlines. The goal is to have our department's budget complete within three weeks. All proposed budgets will be completed by the end of the first week. By Wednesday of week two, the individual budgets will be combined into a departmental budget. At the end of week two we will evaluate the departmental budget in light of strategic goals and the targets set in our initial meeting. All budget revisions must be submitted by Wednesday of the third week. The budget will be finalized at the end of week three.

There are five communication triggers in this budget process: the end of week one, the middle of week two, the end of week two, the middle of week three, and the end of week three. Each of these offers you the opportunity to monitor your team's progress on the budget. Each creates another reason to communicate with your employees.

I'm not suggesting that you constantly look over your employees' shoulders. No one likes that. I'm saying that you have reasons for communicating on each of these dates.

Obviously, you'd prefer to see your employees report to you on those dates. If they don't, you have good reason to follow up with them.

TIP

It's important for your employees to know that you want advance notice if they are having problems. Tell them that you'd much rather take time to help them solve their problems than have them miss the deadline.

If one of your employees fails to tell you that he's having trouble, the communication triggers help minimize the damage, but only if you follow up. Mark the triggers on your calendar, then follow up religiously. You'll save yourself and your employee a lot of unnecessary pain.

Here's another reason for following up. If you don't, you send the message that the deadline is frivolous and you invite the slide of all future deadlines. Employees don't like having their time wasted with deadlines that appear to be whimsical. It's insulting to them and makes you look like a power monger.

TIP

The behavior of others is dictated more by our behavior than by our words. If our words and behavior diverge, others will take their cue from our behavior.

Encouraging Success

We've already discussed the importance of tone in communication. I'm not going to revisit the entire topic again, but I do want to include a reminder here. I cannot emphasize enough the importance of letting your employees know that you want them to be successful.

The more you praise your employees' abilities and encourage their growth, the more likely they are to respond favorably to your leadership. Take advantage of every opportunity to make them feel good about themselves. They'll appreciate you for it and they'll take an interest in your success as well.

The 30-Second Recap

- Good communication is vital to good performance.

- Communication is an aspect of performance that should be evaluated in the appraisal.

- Every personal development plan should include communication skill improvement.

- Performance appraisals allow you, the leader, an opportunity to correct any errors you've made in communicating expectations, providing feedback, or recognizing success.

Lesson 7

Looking at Sample Questions

In this lesson, you will learn about the design of a performance appraisal form and a variety of performance factors; you will also see sample evaluation statements.

Appraisal Form Design

In previous lessons, I discussed performance from a number of perspectives. Now it's time to develop an approach to evaluating the employee's current level of performance.

Even if you aren't involved in the design of your company's appraisal, please don't skip this lesson. There are some valuable insights to be gained even though you may be using an existing form.

Numeric Measures

Most performance appraisals ask for both numeric measures and comments. Here's an example of numeric measures:

How often does the employee meet deadlines?

Never	Occasionally	Usually	Frequently	Always
0	1	2	3	4

Comments:

_____

_____

There are as many variations on this format as there are evaluation designers. Some leaders prefer a 10-point scale. They believe that the larger scale provides greater precision.

Personally, I hated teachers who used pluses and minuses (C+, C, C–) in grading. C+ was disappointing because I just missed a B. C– was distressing because I barely dodged a D. Neither of these grades evokes a positive emotion. That's one of the problems with a 10-point scale. Obviously, I am expressing a personal preference. Your preference is as valid as mine.

I prefer odd-numbered scales, five or seven points, because there is only one number that represents average performance, and that's the *mean* number.

PLAIN ENGLISH

> In a numerical sequence, the **mean** is the number that has an equal number of values above and below it. For example, in the series 3, 5, 7, 9, 11, 7 is the mean because there are two values before it, 3 and 5, as well as two values after it, 9 and 11.

When you have only one number representing "average," it's much easier for the employee to understand the ranking. I prefer a five-point scale, where performance is lousy, below average, average, above average, or great. Most of us find it easy to deal with these concepts. We may not agree with the evaluator, but we understand what she's saying.

In the previous scale, the ratings range from 0 to 4. Many designers choose to use a 1 to 5 scale rather than the 0 to 4 scale. They prefer not to use a 0 rating believing that no one's performance is worthless. I've had one or two employees in 25 years who might refute that argument, but generally it's true. If you have an employee who warrants a 0 rating, I have to ask, "What's she still doing there?"

I use the one-to-five scale for the psychological effect that the "five" rating has. Over the years we've heard about five-star restaurants and five-star hotels. This is the elite class. I want people to believe that they can be elite-class performers. You may think that the employee has nothing to look forward to once she achieves a "five" rating. That's why the appraisal includes a comment section and personal development plan. I never use the "five" rating without raising expectations for future performance. There are, in fact, varying degrees of excellence. You need to make that clear in the development plan and comments.

Another issue in performance appraisal design is whether to use a one-to-five scale or a five-to-one scale, with one being the lowest level of performance and five being the highest.

Some performance appraisal designers feel that people are discouraged when the first measure they see is negative, as it is on a one-to-five scale. Others argue that the positive language of a five-to-one scale may cause the evaluator to be less objective. I don't place much credence in either argument.

TIP

> Whether you like it or not, everything you do or say has a psychological impact. If you're not anticipating the reactions you'll be getting, you're setting yourself up for problems.

I do, however, believe that the evaluator saves time when using the five-to-one scale. Your goal as a people developer is to have your employees score four or five on each question. Why, then, would you want the scale to start at one?

COMMENT SECTION

Now that we've explored the numeric ratings, let's shift our attention to the comment section. Comments are crucial for several reasons.

First, as you decide on a numeric measure you should know why you didn't give this employee a higher evaluation. You need to have a clear understanding of what the next level of performance represents before you can communicate it to your employee. Once you have this understanding, make sure that it is included in your comments.

Your comments should communicate that your employee is building on an already solid base of performance. The language you use is essential for assuring that the appraisal is encouraging, not discouraging. Choose your words wisely.

TIP

Even when you're careful in the selection of your language you can inadvertently offend your employee. If that happens, admit your mistake, apologize, and move on. Your employee will respect your integrity and forgive the offense.

The second reason for using the comment section is that it formalizes your thoughts. Let's face it, the pace of today's world makes it difficult to remember what we did five minutes ago. Don't risk forgetting key elements of your employee's future success; write them down.

Writing down your thoughts is even more important if you take my earlier advice and allow six months between the performance appraisal and the salary review. It can be a challenge trying to remember what you and your employee agreed to six months earlier. You can save yourself a lot of time and avoid the possibility of conflict by capturing your thoughts in the comment section.

A third reason for using the comment section is as an aid in creating the employee's personal development plan. The comments form a ready reference for prioritizing improvement initiatives and establishing an approach to improvement.

Captions for Numeric Measures

Before we move on to examples of performance criteria, there is one more element of performance appraisal design I would like to discuss with you. That's the language that appears above the numeric measures. I've seen all the following:

Excellent	Above Average	Average	Marginal	Poor
Exceptional performance	Exceeds requirements	Meets requirements	Meets most requirements	Fails requirements
Exceptional	Favorable	Satisfactory	Unsatisfactory	Poor
Always	Often	Usually	Sometimes	Seldom
Great	Solid	Okay	Needs improvement	Poor

To me, the captions used for numeric measures are second in importance only to the comment section in appraisal form design. If you doubt that, ask yourself these questions: "How do I feel when my boss says that my work is satisfactory or that it's average? Do I immediately translate the performance evaluation into a personal evaluation? In other words, do I feel that my boss is saying that I'm average or satisfactory?" I'll bet you do. Your employees feel the same way.

My preference is to use the terms *always, often, usually, sometimes,* and *seldom.* These terms are specific to behavior. I've never known them to be used in judgment of an individual as a person.

CAUTION

Some employees are more sensitive than others. These employees tend to view judgments about their performance as judgments of them. You need to be very specific in your language when dealing with these folks.

Now that we have a sense of the form that most appraisals take and the reasoning behind their design, let's look at some of the things you need to evaluate.

PERFORMANCE

In Lesson 1, "The Goals of Performance Appraisal," I discussed four aspects of performance: speed, quality, service, and value. These are not the only factors we might measure, but they form a good foundation on which to build. Let's look at some criteria that can be used to evaluate an employee's performance in each of these areas.

TIP

> The more clearly you define the various aspects of performance, the easier it is for your employees to understand what's expected of them. To help them become successful, be specific when defining performance.

Note: In the interest of saving space, I will not be listing the scale for each of the criteria considered. For the remainder of this lesson, please apply the following scale to the criteria being measured.

Always	Often	Usually	Sometimes	Seldom
5	4	3	2	1

SPEED

Speed is vital to your company's competitive advantage. Here are some statements to help you evaluate your employees' understanding of the importance of speed:

- The employee's actions indicate an understanding of the importance of speed in today's competitive environment.

- The employee does a good job of balancing speed and quality in the performance of his work.

- The employee completes tasks ahead of schedule.

- The employee looks for ways to accomplish routine work more quickly.

QUALITY

Quality cannot be sacrificed for speed. How well do your employees understand this concept? The following statements help you make that determination:

- The employee takes pride in her work.

- The employee does work correctly the first time.

- The employee looks for ways to improve the quality of her work.

SERVICE

The advantages of speed and quality are easily lost to poor service. You can evaluate your employees' service attitude with the following statements:

- The employee's actions indicate an understanding of the importance of serving both internal and external customers.

- The employee demonstrates the desire to serve others well.

- The employee responds to customers in a timely fashion (within two hours).

- The employee provides customers with more than requested.

TIP

Teach your employees how to place themselves in their customers' shoes. It will help them improve their customer service.

VALUE

Understanding value is vital to buying decisions, goal setting, establishing priorities and work effectiveness. Are your employees good at identifying value? The following statements will help you make that judgement:

- The employee's actions indicate an understanding of the concept of value.

- Value is something the employee considers in her decisions.

- When the employee doesn't see value in an effort she makes the appropriate authorities aware of her concerns.

Obviously, there are many more statements that you can use to evaluate these performance criteria. I hope these examples provide you with a good starting point in the development of your evaluation statements.

Next, I'd like you to take a moment to reflect on the previous statements. Did you notice a common thread running through them? They are all positive, aren't they? The language of these statements attributes desirable qualities or behaviors to the employee. The numeric rating indicates the level of quality or consistency of behavior achieved.

Performance appraisals must be encouraging, otherwise the employee will have no desire to improve. The language you use will determine whether your employee leaves the appraisal feeling good and wanting to do better or disappointed and wondering why she should bother trying. The choice is yours. Choose wisely: Your employees' success and your reputation as a people developer are at stake.

OTHER EVALUATION CRITERIA

There are factors that influence employees' performance that aren't directly related to the work they do. These factors are just as important as the factors mentioned above, which means they should be given equal weight in the evaluation process.

INTERPERSONAL SKILLS

The phrase "playing nice with others" is often used in conjunction with "interpersonal skills." With the following statements, you will be evaluating your employees' ability and willingness to consider the needs of others—co-workers, bosses, subordinates, customers, and vendors:

- The employee demonstrates concern for the feelings of others.

- The employee uses language that is encouraging to others.

- The employee willingly helps others.

- The employee genuinely celebrates the success of others.

SUCCESS MENTALITY

"Is the glass half-empty or half-full?" Do your employees "believe" that they can succeed or do they "hope" they can succeed? Here are some statements that will help you evaluate your employees' attitudes toward success:

- The employee possesses a can-do attitude.

- The employee is looking for ways to expand her knowledge.

- The employee is looking for ways to broaden her experience.

- The employee is realistic in her assessment of her abilities.

TIP

> The importance of a success mentality cannot be overstated. None of us can succeed without the belief that we *can* succeed.

OPENNESS TO CHANGE

Many people resist change, others accept it willingly. What are your employees' attitudes toward change? Here are some statements that assist in answering this question:

- The employee willingly accepts change.

- The employee looks for new ways to accomplish old tasks.

- The employee's actions indicate an inquisitive nature.

- The employee views her role as one that is continuously evolving.

CREATIVITY

Creativity can take many forms. Some people are most creative when working with a "blank canvas." Others are very creative when improving existing systems. Still others find their creativity best suited to problem situations. Whatever the arena, creativity is a vital component to your employees' success. Let's look at some statements that are designed to identify your employees' creative talents:

- The employee displays creativity in problem-solving.

- The employee demonstrates the ability to see connections between seemingly unrelated issues.

- The employee can take an abstract concept and develop it into one that's workable.

- The employee applies her creativity to her daily work.

COMMUNICATION SKILLS

In Lesson 6, "Improving Communication," you learned how problems are easily created through poor communication. Here are some statements to use in evaluating your employees' communication skills:

- The employee presents ideas logically in easy-to-understand language.

- The employee voices disagreement without creating conflict.

- The employee writes using clear, concise language.

- The employee uses language that is encouraging.

INITIATIVE

Do your employees initiate improvement efforts or do they wait for someone to assign those efforts to them? Your greatest success, as well as that of your employees, comes when they demonstrate initiative. Here are some statements that will help you evaluate your employees on this vital trait:

- The employee makes herself available to help others when her work is complete.

- The employee seeks involvement in new projects.

- The employee works on skill development outside the workplace.

- The employee is a source of ideas for performance improvement.

CAUTION

If an employee has an extremely hectic schedule for several weeks, and then experiences a slowdown, don't expect her to exhibit the initiative she normally would. She probably needs a little time to rejuvenate herself. Give her that time. Just don't let it become a habit.

PLANNING AND ORGANIZATION

Do your employees plan their futures or react to what the future brings? Can they readily find what they need or do they lose numerous hours each week trying to locate things they need to do the job? The answers to these questions will give you insights into your employees' performance. Here are a few statements that help you assess your employees' planning and organizational skills.

- The employee creates a personal work schedule.

- The employee works the schedule.

- The employee decides on the approach to task before beginning work.

- The employee can easily locate information in her files.

TIP

People who don't have good organizational skills may be in the wrong job. Take a look at their skills and see whether they can be better used in less-structured work.

I hope these criteria and sample evaluation statements will generate even more ideas that you can use in the design of your performance appraisal.

For those of you using existing appraisal forms, I suggest that you evaluate the appraisal language. You may have to alter your verbal communications and write more comments to overcome the appraisal's negative language. Here's an experience I had with an existing appraisal form.

Do you remember my story about the employee who was formulating questions when she should have been listening to instructions? Well, the appraisal form had a statement that dealt specifically with the issue of instructions. The evaluation statement said, "Employee readily understands instructions." I had no choice but to rate her low on this statement. Her failure to listen frequently caused me to repeat instructions.

In the comment section I noted that she needed to listen more carefully and that when she listened to instructions, she had no problems understanding them. When she saw my comment, she thanked me. She said, "This rating makes me sound like I'm retarded, but your comment let me know that you don't feel that way."

Frankly, the word *retarded* is the one that came to my mind when I read the statement. That's why I had so much trouble deciding on a rating. If I hadn't written the comment she would have mistakenly thought that I considered her dim-witted.

Emotions are powerful and they surface very quickly when we feel we're being criticized. When you're completing an appraisal, look for language that might offend your employees. If you find offensive language, use the comment section to remove the sting from poorly designed statements.

360° Feedback

Many companies today are using an appraisal technique called *360° feedback*.

PLAIN ENGLISH

The appraisal system called **360° feedback** is one that elicits appraisals from your boss, your peers, and your subordinates. The term **360°** refers to the fact that you are being evaluated by people all around you. Your boss is above you, your peers are at your side, and your subordinates are below you.

The primary advantage of the 360° feedback system is that it allows multiple perspectives on performance. It also makes it difficult for the employee to dispute her failings when they are being observed by a number of people rather than just her boss.

Everything we discussed in this lesson can be applied to 360° feed-back. You may need to make slight adjustments in the wording of the evaluation statements to reflect differences in perspective between bosses, peers, and subordinates. Otherwise, the approach is the same.

THE 30-SECOND RECAP

- The two most important design components of the performance appraisal are the comment sections and the captions above the numeric measures.

- The captions *always, often, usually, sometimes,* and *seldom* make it more difficult for the employee to translate performance ratings into personal judgments.

- The use of odd-numbered scales makes it easier for both the evaluator and the employee to visualize the concept of "normal" or "average" performance.

- Evaluation statements should incorporate language that indicates success.

- If you are forced to use an existing appraisal form, look for statements that generate negative emotions. Use the comment section to overcome the negative tone of these statements. You may have to adjust your verbal communication as well.

- 360° feedback systems require only slight modifications in the evaluation statements to reflect the differing perspectives between bosses, peers, and subordinates.

Lesson 8

Three Approaches to Performance Appraisals

In this lesson, you'll learn about three of the more common approaches used in conducting performance appraisals.

Approach One: Favors the Evaluator

The most common approach is to prepare the appraisal, invite the employee into your office, give him a few minutes to read the appraisal, then begin a dialogue. I've never felt that this was fair.

As the evaluator, you get to take all the time you want preparing the appraisal, while the employee gets only a few minutes to absorb what you've written before responding. It's particularly unfair to employees who have difficulty thinking on their feet or who are easily intimidated.

Approach Two: A Balanced Approach

Fairness can be built into the system quite easily. Continue to take as much time as you like, but give the employee two working days to review the appraisal and get back with you.

You may be wondering, "Why two days, why not three days or a week?" First, two days is ample time for the employee to reflect on the evaluation and his behavior.

A request for more time is often an indication that he disagrees with your appraisal. If that's true, additional time won't diminish his displeasure. Quite the contrary; given more time, the employee's unhappiness can escalate to anger, bitterness, and resentment. By requiring the employee to discuss his appraisal within two days, you avoid this escalation of ill will.

A second, more selfish reason for selecting two days is that you don't have to reconstruct your thoughts. If more than two days elapse between the completion of the appraisal and the meeting, you may forget some of what you intended to say to the employee. The time spent trying to remember is unproductive. In effect, you're doing the same work twice. If the meeting occurs within two working days, you avoid this waste of time and do a better job of helping the employee.

How do the employees feel about this approach? They like it. First, they don't feel pressured. Second, they have time to organize their thoughts. Third, they have time to reflect on the comments and their own behavior. This approach avoids a lot of the pressure created with "evaluator favored" approach. Here are a few more reasons for adopting this approach.

Regardless of how skilled you become as a communicator, what you say or write can easily be misconstrued. If the employee's gut reaction to your comment is disagreement, the additional time allows him to reread your statement. Often the second reading helps him get past a word or phrase he finds objectionable.

Similarly, a low rating will initially trigger a defensive reaction. Again, the additional time allows the employee to reflect on his behavior. If your rating is accompanied by a comment that illustrates the reason for your rating, the employee will find it easier to accept. Many of the negative reactions we see in performance appraisals can be avoided by simply allowing the employee more time to review the appraisal.

Approach Three: Employee Participation

A friend of mine offered this approach. I haven't had a chance to try it, but I love the concept. She provides the employee with a blank appraisal form and asks him to rate himself. She also asks him to write improvement ideas in the comment section. Simultaneously, she pencils her appraisal of the employee.

At a mutually agreed upon time, they provide each other with copies of the appraisals they've prepared. She allows two days for reflection, then they meet to discuss each item on the appraisal.

CAUTION

When using this approach, you will be tempted to bypass the items on which there is agreement. Don't do it. If you do, you'll forego opportunities to praise your employees and to raise performance expectations for them. These are two integral components of a successful performance appraisal.

There are a couple of advantages to this approach. First, people tend to be more critical of themselves than others are. That means that you'll have opportunities to tell your employee that he's better than he thinks he is. That's a lot more fun than criticizing, isn't it?

Second, you have a chance to reevaluate your ratings. I'm not suggesting that you waffle endlessly on your decisions. That will cost you your employee's respect. I am saying that there are times when new information will influence your thinking.

CAUTION

If you tend to vacillate on decisions or are easily intimidated by an employee, you may find this approach less effective than approach number two.

Approach three opens the door to new information in the form of your employee's perspective. This occurs before the appraisal is finalized. That's why my friend uses a pencil on the initial appraisal; it's easier to make changes when warranted.

The "balanced" and "participative" approaches both provide time for reflection—a critical element in the success of the appraisal. Allow your employees time to think about the ratings, your comments, and their behavior. These approaches remove a lot of the stress normally associated with the appraisal process.

A Few Reminders

The more successful you are at communicating expectations, using communication triggers, and maintaining feedback systems that allow employees to monitor their own progress, the more your ratings and those of your employees will converge.

Agreement is the foundation for future success. Employees who agree with their performance appraisals are open to suggestions for improvement. They are also more likely to act on those suggestions. Their continued success and improvement make all future performance appraisals more enjoyable.

The opposite is true as well. For employees who can't monitor their own progress and who don't get regular feedback, criticism comes as an unpleasant surprise. Employees experiencing these surprises feel that they have been blindsided.

How do you feel about situations like this? Do you want to discuss ideas for improvement? Do you feel that your boss is really interested in your success? I doubt it.

There is another advantage gained by allowing your employees to monitor their own progress. It reduces the amount of time you have to spend on the performance appraisal.

The easier it is for the employee to monitor his progress, the less likely he is to disagree with his evaluation. Appraisal meetings progress more quickly when you don't have to spend time resolving disagreements. You can turn a previously unpleasant task into an enjoyable and rewarding experience by simply creating feedback systems that allow your employees to monitor their progress.

THE 30-SECOND RECAP

- Allow employees two days to review your appraisal before discussing it with you. Most won't take the full two days, but they appreciate the option.

- Have employees rate themselves; often they are more critical of their performance than you are.

- The easier it is for the employees to monitor their progress, the less likely they are to be surprised by the appraisal.

- Fewer surprises result in fewer conflicts. The potential for conflict is what causes us to dread the appraisal process.

LESSON 9
Preparing for the Meeting

In this lesson, you'll learn about some of the things you need to consider in preparing for a successful appraisal meeting.

PROCESS VERSUS PROJECT

First, I want to repeat an important point made in Lesson 8, "Three Approaches to Performance Appraisals." The success of your performance appraisal depends heavily on the things you do during the interval between appraisals. Make sure that you

- Communicate your expectations.

- Use communication triggers.

- Establish feedback systems that allow the employees to monitor their progress.

These tasks, performed well, will do more to create a positive tone for the meeting than anything else you might do. Now let's look at some of the other things that contribute to your meeting's success.

YOUR STYLE

How would you describe your natural style: encouraging, neutral, or critical? If you have a naturally encouraging style, you're fortunate. Setting a positive tone for the meeting will be easy for you. That doesn't mean that you are home free. You've got challenges to overcome, just as managers with other styles do.

First, your enthusiasm can easily be overdone. Excessive enthusiasm is displayed in two ways:

- Ratings higher than warranted by the employee's performance
- Sugar-coating bad news

Who pays the price for these mistakes? Everyone does. Your employee doesn't get the feedback needed to improve. You end up living with substandard performance because you weren't candid in your appraisal. The company doesn't get the performance it needs to remain competitive. There are no winners in this game. If you have a naturally encouraging style, make sure that your ratings and the associated praise are warranted.

TIP

> After you've completed the evaluation, go through each evaluation statement again and ask yourself these questions: "What does this employee need to do to improve performance?" "How much effort will be required: significant, average, or little?" "Does my rating accurately reflect the amount of effort this employee must put forth to improve?"

The neutral style is easier to demonstrate than explain. One of my brothers had a neutral style. When you asked how he enjoyed his vacation he'd answer, "Okay." If you asked about a problem, he'd say, "Not a big deal." Things never got better than "okay" or worse than "not a big deal."

Can you imagine being his employee? You feel like you've done a great job, yet your ratings say your performance is "okay." What a disappointment! At best, you'll feel unappreciated; at worst, betrayed.

Conversely, if your performance stinks, you may not get the feedback you need to improve. Without feedback, you're severely limited in your ability to achieve a secure future.

If your natural style is neutral, you are going to need to find ways to become more encouraging.

TIP

After you've completed the evaluation, go through each evaluation statement again and ask yourself these questions: "What praise can I offer this employee?" "What do I expect from this employee that I'm not currently getting?" "Does my rating accurately reflect the gap between my expectations and the employee's performance?"

If you are critical by nature, you've got a different set of challenges. The success of performance appraisals hinges on your ability to see the good in others and build on that good. That's not natural for you.

It's much easier for you to see what's wrong than what is right. That doesn't mean that you can't see the good; it simply means that you see the bad first. My advice to you is, "Don't fight your nature." Allow yourself your natural tendency, then ask yourself what good you can find in the individual's performance.

TIP

After you've completed the evaluation, go through each evaluation statement again and ask yourself these questions: "Now that I've determined where the employee needs to improve, what has he done right?" "Do my ratings accurately reflect all the good the employee has done?" "How can I make the language I use more positive so that it reflects the results the employee has achieved?" "Are my comments written in a positive or critical tone?"

You'll notice that regardless of the style you possess, I have not asked you to change that style. Rather, I'm offering ways to balance your natural style with the employee's need for an honest and encouraging appraisal.

Is it possible to change your style? Yes, but it often takes years to accomplish. Your style is natural for you, which makes it difficult to change. Does that mean you shouldn't try? Of course not. I believe that each of us needs to strive to become better every day of our lives.

If you choose to change your style, remember that you still have to do a good job today of appraising your employees' performance. Use the balancing techniques I've described until you feel that you've achieved the right blend of encouragement and honest evaluation.

Now that you've evaluated your style, let's examine the impact the employee's style has on the appraisal meeting.

TIP

Just a reminder that both you and your employees will from time to time exhibit all these styles. What you're looking for is the style you or they use most frequently.

EMPLOYEE'S STYLE

Employees also possess one of the three styles just discussed: encouraging, neutral, or critical. Each style poses special challenges in creating the right tone for the meeting.

ENCOURAGING STYLE

An employee who exhibits the encouraging style is upbeat and confident, invites change, and possesses a can-do attitude. The focus of your attention has to be on her realism. Are her expectations of herself and others realistic? Does she often set herself up for failure by being overly optimistic? Is she a good judge of her strengths and weaknesses? Does she only see the good, never the failings?

If the answers to these questions indicate that the employee is realistic, consider yourself lucky. Realistic people appreciate honest, open discussions about their abilities, their potential, and what the future holds for them. Their appraisals will be some of the most enjoyable that you'll experience as a leader.

If the individual is overly optimistic, you've got a little work ahead of you. With overly optimistic employees the challenge is to reign in their enthusiasm without dampening it. You must get them to evaluate their performance more realistically.

Usually, overly optimistic employees expect higher ratings than they get. The disappointment in their ratings will be obvious in their demeanor. This emotional state prohibits the kind of dialogue that's so vital for their future success.

Your ability to predict this reaction is the key to dealing with it. Expect their disappointment. When you know it's coming, you can prepare yourself to accept the reaction without emotion. As long as one of you remains objective, the door remains open for a solution.

Be prepared to tell your employees that you know they are dissatisfied with some of the ratings. Ask where they would have rated themselves higher. Ask for their rationale. Rather than disagree with them, ask them questions that will cause them to view their performance through your eyes. Use questions such as

- What skills would an employee need to get the top rating?

- What should the person getting a top rating be able to do?

- If any employee was accomplishing this level of performance and you knew she had the ability to achieve considerably more, would that alter your rating?

Questions like these cause the employee to consider the ratings more objectively and with less personal attachment.

TIP

Use role-playing. Ask the employee to assume the role of the leader. Ask him questions based on the criteria you used in your evaluation. Then allow him to evaluate the fictitious employee's performance using these new criteria.

NEUTRAL STYLE

Employees demonstrating the neutral style usually won't dispute your ratings unless they are really low. The challenge with these employees is to get them excited about doing more. Often they are quite comfortable with the status quo. Career advancement isn't important to them. They simply want to do a good job, get paid fairly, and enjoy their personal lives.

The key here is to get them to see that job enrichment is an important aspect of total life enjoyment. Your discussions with the neutral types need to focus on how the improvement will make their jobs more fun, not how it will advance their careers.

CRITICAL STYLE

Employees who are naturally critical don't accept criticism well. Often, they are plagued with low self-esteem and little self-confidence. When praised, they tend to discount the praise as flattery because they don't see themselves in that light. I witnessed one case where the employee's self-doubt was so severe that he ascribed selfish motives to the boss's words of encouragement.

Favorable ratings are usually a pleasant surprise to employees who exhibit the critical style. However, the ground gained by these ratings and celebratory comments is often lost when the discussion turns to opportunities for improvement.

TIP

Don't offer performance improvement suggestions to employees who exhibit the critical style. Rather, ask them what would make them better at what they do. Then use their comments as an opportunity to praise both their current performance and their insights into how they might improve.

BLENDING STYLES

Understanding your employee's style will help you anticipate her reactions. The ability to predict behavior gives you a couple of advantages in the meeting. First, it removes the element of surprise that often hinders your effectiveness. Second, when you get the reaction you anticipated, your self-confidence gets a boost and you feel more comfortable. When you're comfortable, it's easier to make your employee comfortable.

Understanding your style allows you to narrow the gap between your style and the employee's. If the employee has an overly optimistic encouraging style and you have a neutral style, you're going to have to increase your enthusiasm so that you don't disappoint the employee.

If your employee has a critical style and you are an encourager, you know that your praise must be well founded or the employee will suspect you of, heaven forbid, flattery. Actually, she'll suspect insincerity, which will cost you credibility in your future dealings with her.

These are examples of why it's so important to blend your style with those of your employees. This is one of the more difficult aspects of performance appraisals. It's also one of the most important to the success of the appraisal meeting.

THE 30-SECOND RECAP

When preparing for the appraisal meeting

- Evaluate your style: encouraging, neutral, or critical.

- Evaluate your employee's style using the same three categories: encouraging, neutral, or critical.

- Use your understanding of both styles to anticipate employees' reactions and plan your responses.

LESSON 10
The Meeting

In this lesson, you'll learn about the psychology at work in an appraisal meeting, as well as techniques and language for improving the emotional climate of that meeting.

FACTORS INFLUENCING EMPLOYEE COMFORT

There is a "natural" psychology that employees experience when entering an appraisal meeting. It's a blend of confidence and fear. Most employees are confident that they've done a good job, yet fear the unknown. Simultaneously, they expect a good appraisal, but wonder if you have an expectation that hasn't been met.

These mixed emotions create discomfort. It's your job to provide comfort at the outset of the meeting. Let's look at some of the factors that influence the employee's comfort.

PARTICIPATION IN SETTING GOALS

If you've allowed your employees to participate in establishing their performance goals, they'll approach the meeting with less fear. Why? Their involvement allows them to feel more secure in their understanding of these goals. Comfort is the companion of knowledge; fear accompanies uncertainty. The level of fear that your employees bring to the appraisal meeting is a function of their knowledge of the goals.

SELF-MONITORING FEEDBACK SYSTEMS

We've already discussed the importance of allowing the employee to monitor his performance. If the employee knows what's expected of him, and the two of you use the same information to monitor his progress, there should be no disagreement about his performance. Again, knowledge removes uncertainty and fear.

Even if your employee knows that he hasn't performed well, he will not experience fear. He doesn't fear low ratings; he expects them. In this situation, you don't have to overcome fear; you have to find out why the fear of failure doesn't motivate this employee. In essence, you have to determine why, in the face of poor performance, this employee didn't change his behavior. Some possible explanations are that the employee

- Doesn't enjoy the work.

- Feels that he has been treated unfairly in the past; poor performance is his way of balancing the scales.

- Is in over his head and lacks the confidence to ask for help.

- Is lazy.

- Dislikes you or your management style.

These are some of the more common reasons why employees ignore the warning signs provided by performance feedback. Are these the only reasons? Certainly not, but I doubt that I could come up with an all-inclusive list if I tried.

TIP

If you find yourself in this situation, begin by exploring the reasons mentioned above. Usually the real reason will surface. Only once in 25 years have I terminated the employment of a poor performer without learning the reason for his failure.

EMPLOYEE SELF-CONFIDENCE

I'm sure it doesn't surprise you to hear that an employee's self-confidence determines the level of fear experienced. We know that people who lack self-confidence are always concerned about what others think of them. Since they feel inadequate, they live in constant fear of disappointing others. So it's natural that the performance appraisal process engenders an inordinate amount of fear for them.

What may surprise you is that even very confident employees experience some fear. Let's be honest. Each of us cares about what others think of us. The possibility that someone may think poorly of us is disconcerting. Oh, I'm sure you've known people who insist that they don't care what others think; you may have even made that statement yourself once or twice. When I hear someone disavow interest in the opinion of others, I'm reminded of the line, "Me thinks he doth protest too much."

The question isn't "Will the employee come to the appraisal with or without fear?" The question is "How much fear will the employee bring to the table?" The employee's level of self-confidence is a good indicator of the amount of fear you should expect.

YOUR STYLE

As we discussed in an earlier lesson, there are significant differences between encouraging, neutral, and critical styles. The farther toward the critical end of the spectrum you are, the more likely the employee is to fear the appraisal meeting. The greater the fear, the more work you have in front of you.

CAUTION

Fear is the single greatest obstacle to an effective performance appraisal.

YOUR APPROACH

In Lesson 8, "Three Approaches to Performance Appraisals," I discuss the following approaches to performance appraisals:

1. Allowing the employee a few minutes in the meeting to review the appraisal before beginning a dialogue.

2. Allowing the employee two days to review the appraisal before initiating the appraisal meeting.

3. Asking the employee to evaluate himself; then allowing two days before the meeting for each of you to review the other's appraisal.

Two of these three approaches allow the employee to privately review the evaluation in advance of the meeting. Employees who have the opportunity to consider the evaluation and prepare their responses are more confident when entering the appraisal meeting. In our discussion of self-confidence we learned that there is an inverse relationship between confidence and fear. The more confidence someone has, the less fear he experiences, and vice versa.

I have noted that fear accompanies uncertainty. Until the employee sees his evaluation, he is uncertain about your opinion of his performance and his future. While you cannot separate fear from uncertainty, you can change the venue for dealing with it.

By permitting the employee to review the appraisal in advance of the meeting, you allow him to deal with his fears privately, rather than in the "public" environment of an appraisal meeting. Most people find it easier to deal with their fears in private than in public. You can remove a lot of the fear from the appraisal meeting by simply allowing the employee to review the evaluation in advance of the meeting.

SETTING THE TONE OF THE MEETING DCF

Now that we have a sense of the psychology at work, let's look at the things we can do to create a better emotional climate. In particular, notice the language that is being used. Modify the language to suit your style or use it verbatim, whichever you prefer. Just make sure that the language is encouraging.

Cause for Celebration

Let the employee know that this meeting is designed to celebrate his accomplishments since the last appraisal and position him for even greater success in the future.

TIP

> After telling the employee that the purpose of the meeting is to celebrate his accomplishments, begin with a recap of his more significant successes. It solidifies the celebratory tone.

Performance Appraisal, Not Personal Appraisal

It's important to let the employee know that you are judging his performance, not him. The more your language focuses on achievements, behavior, and skills, the less likely you are to hurt the individual's feelings. We often hear this advice in parenting classes when we are told to first make sure the child knows he's loved, then tell him how he could have behaved more appropriately. The same concept applies here.

Candor and Disagreement

Two important elements of the appraisal process are candor and disagreement. First, you must be candid with your employees. That means you don't sugarcoat low ratings or offer excessive praise with high ratings. As soon as your language diverges from your beliefs, you lose the respect of your employees.

Similarly, you have to let employees know that you expect candor from them, especially when they disagree with you. Let them know that disagreement is the foundation for future agreement. Assure them that they can disagree with you without fear of retribution. Finally, remind them that you are going to speak only of their performance and not of them as individuals. Tell them that you expect the same consideration when they disagree with you.

Accepting Responsibility

During the performance appraisal, it's not unusual to learn that you've contributed to an employee's performance problems. The natural tendency is to become defensive. Don't! You will gain a tremendous amount of respect from your employees when you take responsibility for your actions.

Ask the employee for ideas on how you can prevent a recurrence of this problem. Reach a conclusion that makes sense to both of you. If the problem is the result of a lifetime habit, ask the employee to remind you whenever he sees you adopting the old habit. Let him know that you will appreciate his help. Not only will you gain the respect of this employee, but more than likely, he'll tell his co-workers of your integrity, and you'll gain their respect as well.

TIP

> Nothing quite elevates an employee's desire to help you succeed as your willingness to credit him for his contributions.

Separating Appraisals and Salary Reviews

Your employee is going to be a lot more open to your suggestions for improvement if he isn't worrying about his salary increase.

Here's what happens when you try to combine salary reviews and performance appraisals. Every time you indicate a need for improvement, the employee is thinking, "What's this going to do to my raise?" With that thought in mind, he can't help but resist or at least trivialize your improvement suggestion.

Contrast that with an improvement suggestion accompanied by the promise of a future salary increase. It's a no-brainer, right? You don't mind accepting new performance targets as long as you will be rewarded financially for achieving those targets. If you want your employees to be open to improvement suggestions and new performance targets, separate the appraisal from the salary review by six months.

JOINT DECISIONS

You didn't get your promotion by seeing problems without seeing solutions. Similarly, you don't see improvement opportunities for your employees without seeing approaches for them to employ. That's as it should be. There are, however, serious dangers involved in telling your employees how to improve.

First, no one likes being told what to do. If you tell your employees what approach they should use to improve performance, they'll resist. It doesn't matter how good your approach is, you will create resistance by requiring them to use it.

The second danger is that your approach may not lend itself to the employee's style. For example, I'm an auditory learner. I learn by listening. If I have an employee who learns by doing and I ask him to use an audio program to acquire new skills, I'm throwing an obstacle in his way. I am asking him to employ a learning style that's unnatural for him. He may be able to acquire the skill this way, but it certainly isn't an effective approach.

TIP

> To get a better sense for how uncomfortable it is to use someone else's approach to a job, try it. Get someone to show you how he approaches a task. Make sure that it's different than the approach you would use. Then perform the task. You'll get a sense of how frustrating it is to do something unnatural.

The third danger is that you might be overlooking approaches that could be even more effective. I have yet to meet anyone who has all the answers. The reality is, there is a plethora of approaches that will work, and we don't know them all.

These are compelling arguments for allowing your employees to choose their own devices for improving performance. Only when you know that their approach won't work, should you intervene in this decision. You owe your employees suggestions on how to improve performance. You also owe them the benefit of your experience and insights in evaluating alternative approaches. You shouldn't, however, make the decision for them. After all, it's the result you're after, not the approach.

TIP
> When people make decisions for themselves, they feel that it's the right decision. That simple reality increases their commitment to the decision.

As you employ the techniques described in this lesson, you'll find that the appraisal meeting is energizing. You and your employees will develop a stronger bond. Together you've set the stage for your mutual success, and that of your company as well.

Your willingness to hear your employees' thoughts, ideas, and opinions will ingratiate you to them. Your ability to admit your failings and your desire to improve serve as models for them.

There is one more very important benefit you'll gain. Future appraisals will be much easier—easier for you because you've become more adept at them, and easier for your employees because they know they're going to be encouraged, not criticized.

THE 30-SECOND RECAP

The "natural" psychology of the meeting is influenced by

- The employees' participation in setting goals.
- The use of self-monitoring feedback systems.
- Employee self-confidence.

- Your style: encouraging, neutral, or critical.

- The amount of time you allow for your employees to review the appraisal before the meeting.

Keys to creating an encouraging atmosphere in the meeting include

- Celebrating employees' successes.

- Appraising performance, not the individual.

- Being candid with your employee and expecting candor from your employee.

- Allowing disagreement without the threat of retribution.

- Taking responsibility when you've contributed to a performance problem.

- Allowing six months to elapse between performance appraisals and salary reviews.

- Permitting the employee to choose his own devices for improving performance.

LESSON 11
Gaining Your Employees' Trust

In this lesson, you'll learn about the importance of trust in the appraisal process. You'll also learn what you need to do to engender your employees' trust.

THE IMPORTANCE OF TRUST

In Lesson 10, "The Meeting," I discuss the importance of candor to the appraisal process. Candor cannot exist without trust. If your employees have any concerns about your motives, they will not trust you.

If you doubt the last statement, recall your experiences with two very different salespeople. The first salesperson gives the impression that her only interest is in the sale. The second demonstrates a genuine interest in helping you make the right decision. Which of the two do you trust? Do you respond as openly to the questions of both salespeople? Of course not!

With the first salesperson, you weigh your responses. You expect her to use everything you say to serve her purpose, making the sale. The way you protect yourself is to withhold information. In other words, your responses lack candor.

Does the second salesperson elicit the same cautious responses? No, your responses are open and honest. In fact, you usually provide more information than the salesperson needs. Why? You know the information will be used to help you, not hurt you.

Your employees react in the same way. When they trust you, they are candid with you. When they don't trust you, they withhold information.

It's virtually impossible for you to succeed in your leadership role when employees withhold information about their fears, interests, goals, and reward preferences. That's why it's so important that you gain your employees' trust.

TRUST—RIGHT OR PRIVILEGE?

A leader's strength is measured by the trust her employees place in her. Trust is not a right; it's a privilege that must be earned every day of your existence. Sadly, trust earned over a period of years can be lost in a few seconds. An ill-chosen word or a senseless act is all that it takes to lose trust.

Fortunately, your employees don't expect you to be perfect. In fact, most employees are very forgiving, if you've earned the right to be forgiven.

Employees forgive mistakes that might otherwise cost you their trust when your past acts and words consistently show you to be worthy of trust. When you normally behave in ways that elicit trust, workers recognize mistakes for what they are. Employees find it easy to forgive the occasional failing. They find it almost impossible to forgive a violation of trust.

Now that we have a sense of the importance of trust, let's see what we have to do to earn that trust.

BE INTERESTED IN THEIR SUCCESS

Your employees must believe that you are genuinely interested in their success. As I tell people in my seminars, "That should be easy. After all, it's you who looks good when your team is successful."

RECOGNIZE THEIR CONTRIBUTIONS

Your employees need to know that you will tout their successes for them. Everyone desires recognition, but most people are reluctant to brag about their successes. By publicly stating your employees' accomplishments you assure them the recognition they deserve without the risk of being labeled a braggart.

Here are some of the benefits you'll realize when you recognize your employees' success:

1. Your employees continue to strive for success.

2. Your employees view you as someone so comfortable with your success that you don't need to "steal" anyone else's.

3. Your employees respect your integrity.

4. Your interest in your employees' success will stimulate their interest in your success.

5. Your employees will be completely candid with you. Their candor makes it easier for you to succeed.

TIP

When presenting an idea, make sure that you credit the employee who came up with the idea. Even if your employee isn't present at the meeting, word will get back to her that you recognized her contribution in front of others. This simple act endears you to your employee and gives her an additional incentive to come up with more ideas. Recognition is a powerful motivator.

CRITICIZE PRIVATELY

While it's important to recognize employees' accomplishments publicly, it's equally important to discuss their shortcomings privately. You know what it's like when someone speaks poorly of you in public. It's embarrassing. You won't gain your employees' trust by embarrassing them in public.

Even though you know better, you can easily fall into the trap of discussing an employee's performance with others. Here are a couple of the more common traps.

You want to vent your frustration before discussing the problem with the employee. The last thing you want to do is begin this type of discussion when you're angry. If that's the case, wait until the end of the day, vent with a loved one who doesn't know the employee, and then go back the next day and discuss the problem with your employee.

At other times, you want the counsel of others on how to deal with this specific performance problem. That's fine, just make sure that you choose counselors who honor confidences. The sting of betrayal will be just as great whether it comes from your lips or those of your advisors.

If you want your employee's trust, discuss her performance only with her and only in private.

TIP

> Remember our earlier discussion of encouraging and critical styles. You are far more likely to see performance improve if you encourage your employee rather than criticize her.

TREAT YOUR EMPLOYEES AS PEERS

How do you feel when someone gives you the impression that she is better than you are? Does the fact that she possesses more talent than you alter your feelings? Absolutely not! An attitude of superiority is insulting even when the individual possesses incredible skills.

It's easy for leaders to develop an attitude of superiority. To understand why, let's assume that your boss just announced your promotion. In effect, she said, "This person has demonstrated abilities greater than those of her peers. I am rewarding her by giving her authority over you." Pretty heady stuff.

Is it any wonder that you feel superior to your new charges? Of course not! If you choose to allow that feeling of superiority to persist, you'll lose your employees' interest in helping you become successful. If,

however, you overcome these feelings, you'll win their respect
and trust.

CAUTION

> If your employees sense that you feel superior, they will
> set you up for a fall. They will find ways to let you know
> that you aren't as good as you think you are.

Avoid Comparing Employees

Your employees need to trust that you won't compare them to their
co-workers. I don't know whether you've ever had your skills or abilities compared to someone else's. I have.

Experience has taught me that in a comparison like this, one person is
treated favorably, the other unfavorably. In other words, there is a win-
ner and a loser. No one likes to be the loser. Even winners cringe at
the comparison. Why? They don't like being used as an instrument of
criticism.

Often, comparisons are made without your realizing what you're
doing. You might make a comparison like this: "Jim has found this
technique to be particularly helpful; you might want to give it a try." I
don't care how pure your motives are, you just told this employee that
his technique isn't as good as Jim's.

Do you trust people who cast you in an unfavorable light? Do you
trust people who repeatedly belittle you by using others to demonstrate your failings? Then use your experience to guide your actions.
Treat each employee as the individual she is.

CAUTION

> When you compare one employee to another you risk
> divisiveness in your department. The employee who
> loses in these comparisons eventually resents the em-
> ployee who wins.

ADMIT WHEN YOU'RE WRONG

Nothing endears you to your employees more than a willingness to admit when you're wrong. You know what it's like to deal with someone who knows she's wrong and won't admit it? You hate it. You also lose respect for the individual. Her actions indicate a lack of integrity. Integrity is an important component of trust, so she also loses your trust. Is that how you want your employees to view you? If not, then be willing to admit when you're wrong.

ALLOW YOUR EMPLOYEES THEIR OWN DEVICES

Micromanagement is a term we hear all too often these days. Those of us who have had the misfortune of working for a micromanager know how frustrating this can be. We'd like to ask, "Why don't you find a machine to do this?" or, "Why don't you do it yourself?"

PLAIN ENGLISH

> **Micromanagement** is the term used to describe a managerial style in which the manager controls minute details of the effort.

You can avoid this reaction by allowing employees to choose their own devices or approaches to doing the work. Here's what the employee "hears" when you allow her to choose the approach:

- "I trust you to do a good job."

- "You know what you're doing; you don't need my help."

- "Your method is as good as mine."

These statements indicate respect for the individual and trust in her abilities and judgment. It's much easier for people to trust you if you trust them. Trust your employees! Leave them to their own devices!

MATCHING WORDS AND ACTIONS

Your words and actions need to match if you want others to trust you. I'm not talking just about the big things; I'm talking about everything.

If you tell an employee you'll help him with a problem later in the day, make sure you help him before the day is out. If you promise to provide information he needs, don't make him ask a second time. If you set a deadline, follow up to make sure the deadline is met.

It's actions like these that tell your employees how good your word is. If your word is your bond, they'll trust you to mean what you say. If you don't honor your word, they'll treat your words as lackadaisically as you do. The choice is yours.

TIP

> When you honor your word, you earn the right to expect others to honor theirs. If you have an employee who isn't careful with the promises she makes, it's much easier to discuss the problem with her when you are modeling the proper behavior yourself.

THE 30-SECOND RECAP

You must earn your employees' trust every day of your existence. The amount of trust you earn is determined by

- Your interest in their success.
- The public recognition you give their accomplishments.
- Your ability to keep their failings private.
- Your success at treating employees as peers.
- Your ability to avoid comparing one employee to another.
- Your willingness to admit to being wrong.
- Your success in avoiding the micromanagement trap.
- Your ability to match your actions to your words.

LESSON 12

Forging Agreements

In this lesson, you'll learn about the types of agreements you need from your employees. These agreements lay the foundation for future appraisals.

LEVELS OF AGREEMENT

Agreement occurs at two levels. *Logical agreement* is the easier of the two to achieve. *Emotional agreement* is more difficult to acquire. It's also more powerful.

> ### PLAIN ENGLISH
> **Logical agreement** occurs when your mind accepts the premise. **Emotional agreement** occurs when you desire to act on the idea.

I'm sure you've had an employee agree with your ideas, yet never act on them. It's frustrating, right? Why didn't the employee act? You achieved only logical agreement; you didn't get to the emotional agreement needed for action.

There is an old sales adage that says, "People buy with their emotions, then justify the decision with logic." Why? We buy emotionally because that's the way we're built. There's no magical insight here; that's just the way we are.

Why do we use logic to justify our decisions? We don't want to appear whimsical or foolish. We're afraid that if we admit to allowing our emotions to rule our decisions our intelligence will be suspect. That's why we use logic to mask the emotions involved in our decisions.

What does this mean to you as a leader? It means that your employees aren't likely to achieve their performance and development goals unless they agree emotionally to those goals. This reality places an additional burden on you. You not only have to get agreement, you have to gauge the level of agreement you're getting.

To help you understand what's involved in getting emotional agreement, let's look at the types of agreement you need.

AGREEING ON YOUR EMPLOYEE'S STRENGTHS

You need agreement on your employee's strengths. This may seem like a ridiculous exercise. After all, the employee knows his strengths, doesn't he? Not necessarily.

Every employee has some tasks that he accomplishes with such natural ease that he doesn't realize that other people struggle with the same work. This is a common occurrence. You need to highlight their strengths to make sure they are aware of them. This awareness is crucial to their ability to teach these skills to co-workers.

TIP

Have your employees share their skills with each other. It's one of the most powerful, inexpensive, and readily available methods for helping your employees achieve their development goals.

When discussing your employees' performance, begin by agreeing on their strengths. It's a wonderful place to start. Not only does it set a positive tone for the meeting, it makes it easy for you to gain emotional agreement very quickly. The more quickly you open the door to agreement, the easier future agreements become.

Discussing Improvement Opportunities

The key to successfully discussing improvement opportunities is to avoid losing the ground gained while discussing strengths. This is not as easy as it might sound. Implicit in the need to improve is an admission that we're not as good as we should be. No one likes to admit that.

The need to improve shouldn't trouble us, but it does. Once again, we're facing the logic-versus-emotion argument. Logically, we know that we're not perfect, that we will never be perfect. Since perfection isn't possible, there is always opportunity for improvement. Intuitively we know this. We can even accept it logically. That doesn't mean we have to like it.

Emotionally, we despise the thought of being less than perfect. We hate admitting shortcomings. The mere thought of inadequacy brings us down emotionally.

Your employees wrestle with the same emotions we do. It is easy to trigger these emotions in your employees by using the wrong language in discussing improvement opportunities. Once lost, the emotional high gained from reviewing strengths is almost impossible to regain. How can you be sure that you're using the right language? Avoid discussing "the need to improve." Rather discuss the "desire to improve."

Here are some examples of language you can use:

- Instead of asking, "How do you think you can improve your skills?" ask, "What's the next level of success you want to achieve with these skills?"

- Rather than ask, "What are your weaknesses?" ask, "How can you build on your strengths?"

- Don't ask, "Why do you struggle with this type of work?" Ask, "What would make it easier for you to accomplish this task?"

You get the picture.

When discussing improvement opportunities, you can either build on the momentum gained in your discussions of strengths or lose that momentum through ill-chosen words. The choice is yours.

CAUTION

> There are lots more agreements to gain. Drop the ball at this early stage, and you've set yourself up for a long, difficult, and often unproductive appraisal meeting.

APPROACHES TO IMPROVEMENT

Once you've achieved emotional agreement on what needs to be improved, you and your employee have to agree on the approach to use. In an earlier lesson we spoke of the importance of leaving employees to their own devices. Let's revisit the emotional aspects of leader-directed versus employee-directed approaches.

Place yourself in the role of the employee. Let's assume that you and your boss have decided that you need to become more organized. Last year your boss attended a wonderful seminar on organization skills. He suggests that you attend the seminar.

You don't like group education. You prefer audio programs for several reasons. First, you feel that you learn better in a quieter environment. Second, you aren't the type of person who likes to participate in exercises, nor do you ask a lot of questions. Third, you enjoy the ability to rewind and review anything that didn't quite register the first time. Finally, you consider yourself a slow learner. It's not that you are stupid, it's just that sometimes it takes a little longer for you to grasp a concept than it does your co-workers.

Now let's assume that your boss insists that you take the seminar. What's your commitment likely to be? Are you likely to postpone action on this approach? If you do agree to attend the seminar, will your agreement be logical or emotional? How will the level of your agreement affect the benefit you gain from the seminar? How likely is it that your organizational skills will improve? The answers are obvious.

Am I suggesting that you give your employees carte blanche? Absolutely not! When you see that your employee's approach isn't going to work, you have a duty to convince him that it won't work. It's your job to prevent his failure.

Again, be precise in the language you use. Don't say, "That won't work." A statement like this puts the employee on the defensive. You know the odds of gaining emotional agreement when the employee is being defensive.

You're better off asking, "What's this approach going to do for you?" By using this question you get the employee to reexamine his decision. If you're right and he has overlooked something important, he will find the mistake during his analysis. If he doesn't see his error, ask follow-up questions that allow him to examine aspects of the decisions he hasn't considered. When he realizes his error he'll abandon his approach in favor of one that holds out the opportunity for success.

There are two keys to gaining emotional agreement on approaches:

- Allow the employee to choose his own devices.

- If the employee's approach won't work, use leading questions to help him reach the conclusion that it won't work.

MEASURES OF IMPROVEMENT

When it comes to measuring improvement, emotional agreement hinges more on the *amount of improvement* than on the *performance measure* used.

PLAIN ENGLISH

Amount of improvement relates to the level of success. Should the desired level of improvement be 10 percent, 30 percent, or 70 percent? **Measures of performance** include speed, number of defects, number of errors, and volume produced.

It's much easier for the employee to agree on the measure to be used than on the amount of improvement to be targeted. The key here is realism. Employees tend to be more conservative in their estimates than leaders do. Why?

First, employees are the ones who are committing to the goal. Since no one wants to fail, they naturally become cautious. Second, depending on your style, they may get the idea that you're trying to build a career on their results and you really don't care how it affects them. Third, there is the confidence issue. Some employees don't possess confidence commensurate with their skills. In other words, they underestimate their own abilities.

You have a much better chance of achieving emotional commitment to improvement measures if you ask your employees

- For their estimate of what's realistic.

- What obstacles stand in the way of greater improvement.

- To help devise a plan for overcoming these obstacles.

Their participation in this process is the key to gaining emotional agreement.

If you're working with an employee whose fear simply won't allow him to agree to the performance measure you need, there is one more approach you can try. It's worked well for me when I've had an extremely cautious employee.

The approach, which is detailed below, is a combination of statements and questions that are designed to elicit agreement. Once again, pay particular attention to the language. The language is designed to help the employee remove the emotional constraints imposed by his comfort zone. Here's the approach:

- I know that I'm asking you to stretch beyond your comfort zone.

- I realize that you don't want to fail.

- I don't want you to fail either.

- If we agree that this lower level of performance is acceptable, will you try to achieve the higher level?

- I promise you that missing the higher target won't negatively impact your next appraisal or your salary.

- Achievement of the higher goal can, however, improve your next appraisal and offers the benefit of a higher increase.

- I know that you have concerns about the more aggressive target, but I believe that you can achieve it.

CAUTION

> You have to walk the talk. You cannot express disappointment, withhold praise, or adjust the salary increase because the employee doesn't hit the more aggressive target. If you do, you violate his trust. Trust lost is difficult to regain.

My experience is that when I take the pressure off employees and state confidence in their abilities, they typically achieve the more aggressive goal. To me, that's proof of their emotional commitment to the goal.

DEADLINES FOR IMPROVEMENT

All the same fears and concerns that we discussed with improvement measures hold true for deadlines. When you develop the skills to deal with one, you equip yourself to handle both.

REWARDS FOR IMPROVEMENT

In particular, you want to gain agreement on the amount of increase that the employee will receive if he achieves his goals. The "amount" can be a percentage increase over his current base pay.

The key here is to emphasize the relationship between performance improvement, the value of the improvement, and the amount of increase. The clearer the employee's understanding of the value gained by the improvement, the less likely he is to demand unrealistic increases. People understand the concept of value. They employ it every day in their buying decisions. They also understand that the company is purchasing their services. If, for some reason, the employee forgets this simple fact, don't hesitate to remind him.

By using this value approach, you'll gain another valuable insight into your employee's character. How? You'll learn his definition of fair.

An employee who is greedy will ask for a disproportionate share of the value he generates. His willingness to "settle" for less depends on the importance he places on money and the presence of other aspects of job satisfaction.

CAUTION

Be aware that employees who "settle" for less than they want often balance the scales by reducing performance. That's contrary to your goal of improving performance.

For most employees the importance of salary declines if

- There is significant investment in their education.

- They have a sense of being a part of something bigger than themselves.

- Their ideas are welcomed and acted upon.

- Their contributions are recognized publicly.

- They can choose their own devices in accomplishing goals.

- They like their leader.

Those of you who have taken a job for more money and later found these satisfaction factors missing know exactly what I mean.

By providing more of the intangible aspects of job satisfaction you minimize the importance of money for most employees. This makes it easier for the two of you to agree on monetary rewards.

THE 30-SECOND RECAP

- Agreement must occur at the emotional level if it's going to drive action.

- Without action there is no improvement. Your employees' development depends on your ability to gain their emotional agreement.

- Areas in which you need agreement are the employees' strengths, improvement opportunities, approaches to improvement, measures of improvement, deadlines for improvement, and rewards.

LESSON 13

Feedback Systems and Recognition Programs

In this lesson, you'll learn about feedback systems and recognition programs for various areas of the operation.

FEEDBACK SYSTEMS—THE MISSING LINK

Feedback is the often-overlooked component of performance improvement. This may seem strange, but it's true. To help you understand how this happens, let's look at a typical exchange between leader and employee.

You're the leader. You and your employee agree that you want to reduce the cycle time on billing by two days. You also agree that the employee's focus is going to be on procedures rather than on technology. Both of you feel that the goal can be achieved within two months. Your employee leaves the meeting ready to begin the procedural analysis.

What's missing? Deadlines? Communication triggers? Progress reports? Essentially, you and your employee failed to establish a feedback system. Why didn't it get developed?

Very simply, the existence of an agreement and your trust in your employee cause you to overlook the need for a feedback system. When your employee leaves the meeting you are convinced that she

- Has a clear understanding of what needs to be done.
- Understands the importance of the improvement initiative.

- Knows the deadline and its importance.

- Will honor her agreement to achieve this goal.

Wouldn't life be grand if it worked that way? The reality is that during the two months preceding the project's due date, this employee

- Has a "normal" workload to complete.

- Will certainly encounter problems in dealing with the "normal" workload.

- Will be asked to participate in new initiatives.

- Will make numerous priority decisions regarding work flow.

- May have to deal with family crises.

- May have to fill in for absent employees.

In other words, there are a lot of things that can distract your employee from the agreed-upon goal. You can help her remain focused on the goal by establishing a feedback system. Here's an example of a simple feedback system:

- **Week two:** The employee submits procedural changes that have the potential of reducing the billing cycle by two days.

- **Week four:** The employee presents the reactions of employees who will be affected by the changes.

- **Week six:** The employee provides procedural updates including oral and written communications to the affected employees and launches the improvement effort.

- **Week eight:** The employee reports on the early stage success, the obstacles confronted, and the solutions created.

TIP

> Your feedback system needs to align specific results with a very clear deadline to be effective.

The existence of these interim goals and deadlines intensifies the employee's focus throughout the two-month time frame. This simple step dramatically improves the employee's odds of being successful. If the employee becomes distracted and loses sight of this goal, you'll know it much sooner. You'll also be able to take corrective action much earlier than you would without the feedback system.

I know that we've discussed this before, but it bears repeating. When you establish a feedback system, be sure that the employee can monitor her progress. In the feedback system just outlined, you can see that it's easy for the employee to determine whether she

- Identified procedural changes.

- Obtained the reactions of affected employees.

- Provided written procedures and oral instructions to each affected employee.

- Obtained information on the success and problems her coworkers experienced.

- Met the deadlines.

Now that you have a sense for the more common mistakes made with feedback systems, let's look at a variety of operating areas and determine what your feedback systems can measure.

MARKETING

There are two goals in marketing. The first is to create general market awareness; does the public know that we exist?

That's why you see pharmaceutical companies running ads touting their prescription medications. It's also the reason why you see the "Intel Inside" logo on every computer that includes Intel chips.

The second goal of marketing is to elicit orders. General awareness ads run by a pharmaceutical company won't influence the physician who is making the buying decision. He needs study results, drug interaction information, a clear understanding of possible side effects, and the cost of the medication. It's obvious that these marketing goals require different approaches and, consequently, different feedback measures.

GENERAL AWARENESS MARKETING

Let's use the pharmaceutical company example. The company is marketing a cholesterol-reducing prescription medication. How will the company determine the success of its general awareness ads? What feedback systems can it employ?

1. The company can survey people within the age group that is at greatest risk of heart disease. These people are likely to have their cholesterol tested on a regular basis. The company's survey can include questions like:

    *   Are you familiar with the names of these medications? (Provide a list that includes your medications and those of your competitors.)

    *   What is the purpose of each of these medications?

    *   Based on the ads you've seen, which medication would you consider most effective?

    *   Would you ask your physician about this medication if you had high cholesterol?

    *   If you had a loved one who had high cholesterol, would you suggest that she ask her doctor about this medication?

    This information will tell the marketing people how successful they are in gaining public interest in their products.

2. The company can survey physicians with questions such as:

    *   What percentage of your patients with high cholesterol asks about a specific medication?

- Which cholesterol-reducing medications are generating the most interest with your patients?

- Which medication produces the most inquiries? Which medication ranks second? Third?

- Do patients who inquire seem to have a preference for one medication over another? If so, what's the reason for their preference?

Measurements from the physicians' survey may be less precise than the public survey. That's because doctors don't often track the frequency of patient requests for a medication. They do, however, remember their patients' questions. That's enough to help the pharmaceutical companies gauge the effectiveness of their market awareness campaign.

TIP

> Make sure you understand the level of precision that exists in the measures you use. A lack of precision doesn't eliminate value, but it may diminish value.

With the information from these two surveys, the marketing team can assess its current level of success and establish goals for improvement. Assume that the surveys show that 37 percent of the public knows the name, but only 8 percent ask their physicians about the product.

There are several improvement opportunities available. The marketing team can pursue an increase in public awareness from 37 percent to, let's say, 40 percent. It can target higher rates of patient inquiry off the existing 37 percent awareness. Or the marketing group may pursue some combination of the two. The feedback from the initial effort provides the basis for new goals, new marketing messages, and new feedback. That's the cycle of continuous improvement worth employing.

ORDER ELICITING MARKETING

Some of the things you want the feedback system to track are

- The number of contacts with the physician before an order is received.

- A ranking of the physicians' concerns about the medication; this information can reduce the number of contacts needed.

- Whether physicians respond most often after a mail piece, a phone call, an office visit, or attending a seminar.

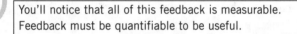

TIP

You'll notice that all of this feedback is measurable. Feedback must be quantifiable to be useful.

SALES

There are many activities involved in selling, most of them are easily quantified. Here are some feedback measures used in sales management:

- Number of telephone contacts in a day.

- Number of appointments made in a day.

- Number of appointments cancelled or postponed each day.

- Percentage of appointments that result in sales on the first call, second call, and so on.

- Average size of the sale.

- Profit margin on the sale.

- Percentage of sales that come from existing customers versus new customers.

CAUTION

Averages can be misleading. When evaluating the average size of the order or the average profit margin, make sure that you understand the magnitude of the range included in the averages.

PRODUCTION

Production efficiency involves a lot of measures including quality, speed of delivery, material costs, labor costs, equipment costs, error rates, and rework costs. Here are some measures that address the various aspects of production:

- Material costs.

- Your vendors' defect rate on parts supplied.

- Time required for each phase of production.

- Reject rates.

- Rework costs.

- Percentage of shipments that go out early, on time, or late.

- Number of units produced by shift.

- Number of shipments returned by customers.

- Credits given to customers for poor quality.

If you're experiencing high numbers on the last two items, you've got some serious problems. It's probably the result of not having feedback on the other items in the list.

CREDIT AND COLLECTION

You want your credit and collection function to strike a good balance between increasing business and improving cash flow. The following measures will help you achieve that goal:

- The percentage of "new customers" who don't qualify for credit; this will give you insights into whether your sales force is targeting the right customers.

- The percentage of customers who are delinquent.

- The dollar amount of delinquent receivables.

- Which industries produce the highest level of delinquency.

- Which customers represent the greatest percentage of delinquent receivables.

- How many collection calls your staff makes in a day.

- How many calls it takes to collect the money.

- What percentage of receivables get sent to outside collection services.

- The amount spent on outside collection services.

- Which outside collection service is most effective.

CAUTION

Collection is one area of operation in which you need to pay particular attention to how improvement affects the customer. If further shortening of the collection period is going to irritate customers with good payment histories, it's not a worthwhile improvement.

HUMAN RESOURCES

Human resources is responsible for the hiring, retention, and development of good performers. Mistakes in any of these areas are very costly to the organization. The following measures can be used to evaluate the human resource function's performance:

- Employee turnover rate.

- Cost of hiring an employee.

- Cost of terminating an employee.

- Length of time required for hiring a new person.

- Percentage of new hires that leave after a month, three months, six months, a year.

- Employee participation in discretionary training offered by the company.

- Effectiveness of training.

- Number of grievances filed.

- Win/lose percentages on grievances.

- Number of grievances filed against each leader.

- Types of grievances filed.

TIP

> To gain greater insights into how to evaluate training, read Donald Kirkpatrick's book *Evaluating Training Programs, The Four Levels.*

FINANCE

One of the finance group's responsibilities is reporting financial information to operating managers and the general public. The finance group is also charged with paying bills and monitoring the company's cash situation. Here are a few items that the finance group might track to measure its performance:

- Number of days required to provide financial statements to operating managers.

- Number of adjustments required before publishing the financial statements.

- Number of corrections required after the statements are published.

- Cost of processing vendor invoices and paying bills.

- Cost of billing customers and making deposits.

- Number of transactions processed per person.

- Cycle times involved in handling receivables and payables.

- Timeliness of expense reimbursements.

Certainly, these are not all-inclusive lists. Nor do they cover all areas of operation. There are many more measures that can be tracked in each of these feedback systems.

The keys to a successful feedback system are as follows:

- A specific performance goal exists.

- The goal must be measurable.

- Results must be posted frequently, preferably daily.

- Results should be posted where the work is done and in high-traffic areas.

- Each employee is able to gauge his contribution to the result.

One of the greatest benefits you'll gain from a feedback system is focus. With all the demands made on us and our employees, it's easy to lose sight of what's important. Feedback systems provide focus and the means to maintain that focus every day.

TIP

> In my 25 years of experience in leadership roles, I've found that the reason more people aren't successful is that they lose focus. Feedback systems allow you to help your employees retain the focus they need without having to continuously look over their shoulders.

RECOGNITION PROGRAMS

Feedback guides success, recognition rewards success. Some say that success is its own reward. There is some merit to that statement, but the greater reward lies in recognition. Think about the satisfaction you feel when you achieve a goal. Now compare that feeling with the one you get when someone comes to you and says, "I just heard that you cut two days out of the billing cycle. That's incredible."

Which of these two "rewards" is more enjoyable? The latter, right? That's why it's so important to build recognition programs into your daily activities.

It may seem that we are drifting away from the performance appraisal topic, but we aren't. Remember, the goal of the performance appraisal is to help employees become more successful. That success isn't going to occur unless you help them stay focused on their goals, allow them to monitor their performance, and recognize their accomplishments during the interval between appraisals. Now that we see how recognition programs fit into the appraisal process, let's look at different approaches to recognition.

I've seen organizations post employees' accomplishments on bulletin boards, banners, and, yes, in the electronic age, on the company's *intranet.*

PLAIN ENGLISH

Intranet is a software network similar to the Internet except that its access is limited to the company's employees, customers, and vendors.

Some companies offer financial incentives, cash awards, trips, sports tickets, merchandise, or vehicles. The possibilities are endless. Others give gag gifts to add another dimension of fun to the celebration.

Still others bring in pizza or ice cream so that the whole team can join in the celebration. A reward that employees really enjoy is getting out early on a Friday afternoon. If my team had an unusually successful week, I'd send them home at 3:30 or 4:00 in the afternoon. It's amazing how much longer the weekend seems when you miss rush-hour traffic.

The form of recognition isn't as important as being recognized. Your employees know you care about them when you make time to celebrate their successes. The more that you demonstrate your interest in their welfare, the more they'll care about yours.

CAUTION

In Lesson 4, "Striving for Employee Satisfaction," I discuss the importance of recognizing an employee's personal best. The tendency is to recognize only top performers. If you recognize only your top performers, you risk having the majority of your employees lose interest in improving their performance.

THE 30-SECOND RECAP

- Feedback is essential to performance improvement. Good feedback systems provide information that is quantifiable, timely, and easily monitored by both you and your employee.

- Feedback is essential for helping employees maintain focus on their goals. Lack of focus is the primary cause of missed goals. In effect, feedback guides success.

- Recognition is the reward for a job well done. It's essential to the employees' ability to remain motivated during the time between performance appraisals.

- The more opportunities your employees have to celebrate success, the more they'll desire success. After all, everyone loves to celebrate.

LESSON 14

You Can't Win 'Em All

In this lesson, you'll learn that regardless of how adept you become at performance appraisals, some just won't take.

THE PROBLEM

First I want to share my attitude toward performance. I believe that employees have to do more than their "job." They have to find ways to do the job more effectively. Whether you agree or disagree with that definition, my employees know that's what I expect of them.

Not all performance appraisals produce the results that you desire. Read on to learn about one of my more glaring failures ….

I had an employee who wasn't performing to expectation, yet she wanted a double-digit salary increase. These were the days before I learned to separate appraisals and salary reviews. Now that I think about it, this appraisal may have been the reason I separated the two.

This employee did her "regular" work well. The problem was that whenever I asked for anything new from her, she responded, "I can't do that." When I asked why not, she'd say, "It's too complicated for me." I reminded her that she had handled more complicated tasks in the past, but she insisted that my new requests were beyond her abilities.

One day I overheard her telling some of her coworkers how wonderful her husband was. She said, "Last night I was going to help him with the lawn. He told me that it was too hard for me, that he would take care of it." She went on to describe several other situations in which her husband did the work because it was "too difficult" for her. She admitted that she enjoyed being pampered in this way.

Obviously, this arrangement was working well for them in their marriage. That's great! It's not my place to tell others how their marriages should work. At the same time, I can't allow one employee to get by saying it's too hard without offering the same consideration to all employees.

As you can imagine, the appraisal meeting wasn't much fun. She contended that she was doing a good job on the work she had been assigned. I agreed, but reminded her that I had always expected continuous improvement. She said that anything more than what she was currently doing was just too difficult. I retorted by saying that I thought she was underestimating her abilities. She disagreed.

This discussion went on for more than an hour with no progress. I suggested that we postpone our discussion until after lunch. I expressed my hope that the break might help us resolve our differences. When I came back from lunch her appraisal was on my desk. Across the front of the appraisal, in big red letters, she had written, "Bull——!" She never came back from lunch.

I'm not proud of this result. I wish that I could have found a way for us to reach an agreement. My reason for sharing this failure is simply to help you understand that you won't always be successful. There are many reasons why the appraisal process fails.

TIP

> When you strive for perfection you become more successful. When you expect perfection, you set yourself up for failure.

WHEN AN EMPLOYEE DOESN'T VALUE PROFESSIONAL GROWTH

Some employees aren't interested in a career. All they want is a job that pays well enough to allow them to enjoy their leisure time. I've done a lot of work in the construction industry. I can tell you that when deer season opens, even foremen call in sick if they can't get time off any other way.

Other employees lose the desire to grow when their careers reach a plateau. Sometimes that plateau is a personal choice. They enjoy the work and don't want to advance beyond that point.

Often the decision is made for them. They are passed over for promotions, and they realize that regardless of how much effort they put forth they aren't going to rise to the next level. These employees suffer from a malady known as "retirement on the job." It's difficult to regain the interest of someone who has the attitude, "Why bother?"

Lifestyle changes also influence the employee's attitude toward growth. In the example of my failure, marriage encouraged the employee's attitude of "it's too difficult." Chronic health problems often rob a person of his desire for career growth. So can a large inheritance, winning the lottery, or simply getting older. All of these factors influence the employee's desire for personal growth.

POOR MORALE

A promotion often includes inheriting a staff. The good news is you don't have to scramble to find people, and you have lots of experience from which to draw. The bad news is you may inherit morale problems.

Twice in my career I "inherited" people who felt that

- They were the dumping grounds for all the nasty work in the company.

- No one appreciated their contributions.

- Their salaries weren't adequate.

It's virtually impossible to turn around an employee with these beliefs. If you've found an effective way to do this, call me. In 25 years, I have not found a remedy for this malady.

TIP

Don't assume that an employee with poor morale is experiencing these feelings. There are other causes of morale problems that can be cured.

CONFIDENCE

I discuss the importance of confidence in Lesson 3, "Encouraging Employee Development," Lesson 9, "Preparing for the Meeting," and Lesson 10, "The Meeting." If an employee possesses low self-esteem and little confidence, the appraisal process is going to be difficult. Still, I'd much rather deal with a confidence problem than with the morale issue. Why? I have a chance at success when dealing with confidence problems; I don't with morale.

You see, with confidence, I can structure the work so that the employee experiences a series of successes. With each success comes confidence. Only if the employee lacks the confidence to try do I have an insurmountable problem. Other than the failure I described earlier, I've never met an individual who wasn't willing to try at some level.

WHEN AN EMPLOYEE DOESN'T ENJOY WORK

In recent years we've seen a significant increase in the number of workers expressing interest in changing careers. I doubt that the interest itself is new, rather I believe that several cultural changes encourage employees to act on their interests.

One change is the workers' attitude toward security. Most employees no longer view security as lifetime employment with one company. The plethora of *mergers* and *downsizings* of the past two decades have taught workers that they can't rely on the company for employment, they have to depend on their abilities. So many people have lost jobs in recent years that the stigma once associated with frequent job changes is gone.

PLAIN ENGLISH

> **Mergers** occur when two companies combine into one.
> **Downsizings** are significant reductions in a company's
> workforce. They usually represent a cost-cutting move.

Education is another important ingredient. Our workforce is one of the
best educated in the world. Many people, especially those in midlevel
management positions, find that their skills and knowledge have appli-
cation well beyond their current jobs. The transferability of their skills
makes career changes easier. If your employee is serious about wanting a career change, it's going to be difficult to interest him in improving performance in his current job.

Obviously, each of these situations threatens your success in helping
your employees improve performance. How do you deal with them?

First, avoid the temptation to act as a parent. As parents, we instruct
children about what's right. That's fine for children; they don't have a
great deal of experience to draw upon. For an adult it's condescending.

You know how much you resist the attempts of others to treat you like
a child. Your employees will react the same way. If you adopt a parental mindset with your employees, your attempts to help them will
almost certainly fail.

THE SOLUTION

Now that I've discussed what not to do, let's look at each of the previous situations with a focus on success.

WHEN AN EMPLOYEE DOESN'T VALUE PROFESSIONAL GROWTH

You can generate or rekindle interest in professional growth by asking
the employee what he and his family would do with extra income. Get
him to dream. The more he thinks about what he wants, the easier it is
for you to tie performance improvement to those dreams.

TIP

> This approach is useful for all employees. The more you frame what you want in terms of what they want the more likely you are to get action. With workers who've lost interest in their work, it's mandatory.

I realize that this approach isn't going to work with employees who win the lottery or receive large inheritances. Frankly, you don't have to worry about improving their performance; they're not likely to remain in your employ.

POOR MORALE

As I said earlier, if you have an effective way of dealing with the employee's perception of years of mistreatment, please let me know. I haven't found the answer. The best I've been able to accomplish is to guide them to leave on their own.

You'd think that it would be easy to convince an employee with morale problems to leave, but it isn't. Why? The employee is already pessimistic about the future. He's been treated poorly in the past, and he has no reason to believe that will change.

When he considers other employment, his negative frame of mind causes him to look for the things that could go wrong in another job, not at what might be good about that job. That's why these employees tend to resist help in finding other work.

Your only alternative may be to discharge the employee. If you can't get him turned around in a couple of months, make the decision and move on. You'll both be better off. If you doubt that, let me remind you that I inherited two people with precisely these attitudes. In both cases, I had to fire them. They were both extremely angry with me for adding to their problems. In both cases, these people saw me about a year later, came up to me, and thanked me for letting them go. They had both found jobs that they enjoyed and were making more money than before.

In both cases, I experienced mixed feelings. Simultaneously, I was happy for them and angry with them. I was happy to hear that they were enjoying their work again. They were good people with the skills necessary to do a very competent job.

At the same time, I resented the fact that they didn't leave on their own. I hated having to be the one to make the inevitable decision. I wished they had made it on their own. Now I realize that their feelings of unfair treatment caused them to have a pessimistic attitude toward life. I can see that it would have been very difficult for them to overcome this pessimism and make the decision they needed to make. If you ever find yourself in this situation, I hope you'll remember my experiences and make the difficult decision. You really are helping your employee as much as yourself.

CONFIDENCE

We've already discussed the handling of confidence issues. The only thing I would add is that if the employee is so deficient in confidence that he's unwilling to try, you need to suggest counseling. The individual needs the help of a trained professional.

Even if you have the training necessary to counsel the employee, I recommend outside professional help. Why? The time required to help this person will prevent you from helping the rest of your employees become more successful. It's simply not fair to penalize them for another employee's problems. Use outside professional help for really difficult situations.

CAUTION

> Don't confuse caution with confidence. Some employees are very thorough because they want to be sure they understand what's expected of them. That's caution, not lack of confidence.

WHEN AN EMPLOYEE DOESN'T ENJOY WORK

If the employee has lost interest in his work, find out what interests him now. I'm assuming that this employee was, at one time, a productive worker. Make sure that the new interest is not just a passing fancy, but a sincere desire to fill an emotional need in his life.

Once you ascertain the genuineness of his desire, look within your department for work that might meet his needs. If you can't provide the opportunity he wants, assure him that you'll help him look elsewhere within the company to accommodate his needs. It's better to lose a good worker to another department than to lose him to another company, especially if that company ends up being a competitor.

When you help him find a job in another department, arrange a trial period for both your employee and his new leader. Why? I've seen too many employees who thought a job would be "fun" learn very quickly that it isn't. Leave the door open. If the new job doesn't work, not only will your employee be grateful to have his old job back, he'll be very interested in improving his performance. The new leader will be glad that he doesn't have to decide what to do with an unhappy employee.

TIP

When discussing a trial period for the new job, agree on a reasonable time frame. Remind him that your team can't work shorthanded forever, nor can the new leader afford to invest in an employee who may not remain with the department.

CAUTION

Don't allow your employee to decide frivolously that he wants to try something new. That's a formula for chaos. It's easy to tell whether or not he's sincere. If there's passion in his voice, a sparkle in his eye, and he becomes animated as he describes his newly found interest, he's sincere.

There is one last piece of advice I have for situations like those just described. Don't spend an inordinate amount of time with poor performers. When you do, you diminish your ability to help those who have earned the right to benefit from your time and talents.

Good performers deserve success. It's your job to see to it that they enjoy success for many years to come. You can't do that, baby-sit poor performers, and plan for the future. There simply aren't enough hours in the day. Use your time wisely; spend most of it with your good performers.

I'm sure some of you are wondering, "How do I minimize my time with poor performers? After all, they are the ones causing me the most problems." Here's an approach that's always worked well for me:

1. Set expectations, with or without his agreement.

2. Establish deadlines, with or without agreement.

3. Create a self-monitoring feedback system.

4. Tell the employee that the ball is in his court; he can choose to produce or not as he sees fit.

5. Let the employee know that his choice will determine his future employment.

You won't believe how liberated you'll feel when you place the responsibility for the employee's future employment where it belongs, with the employee.

Another reason for using this approach is the impact it has on the rest of the team. You win the respect and support of good employees when they see that you aren't

- Wasting time with an unwilling worker.

- Shifting work to them that should have been done by a poor performer.

- Tolerating ill-humor or poor performance.

- Hesitating to eliminate a poor performer who refuses to get with the program.

Even though employees know that life isn't fair, most of them like to see some measure of equity in the workplace. It allows them to feel good about themselves and the environment in which they work. The approach I've just outlined gives your employees a sense that you're fair in your dealings.

There are other advantages to this approach. Employees who feel that everyone is being treated fairly are more productive. For one thing, they don't spend their days trying to figure out how to balance the scales.

I've seen people who wouldn't think of taking a paper clip from the office, slow their production because they didn't feel they were being compensated fairly. There's no malice intended, it's a natural reaction to the perception of inequity.

TIP

> Employees who are balancing the scales are often un-aware of what they're doing. If you see this happening, help your employee see the error of this strategy, then work together to remove the inequity they perceive.

Another advantage of this approach is that employees who feel they are being treated fairly approach their work with greater verve, which increases their productivity, and with it their performance. All of these advantages come from placing the responsibility for the poor performer's employment where it belongs, on his shoulders.

THE 30-SECOND RECAP

- Try to find out why an employee doesn't have an interest in improving performance.

- If the employee lacks confidence or has become bored with the work, you can often salvage the employee. To deal with a lack of confidence create a plethora of opportunities for the employee to succeed. Each success will build confidence. For the bored employee, add some variety to his work.

- If the employee's attitude toward the company is poor or if he has simply lost interest in the work, you're probably going to have to help him find other employment.

- One of the biggest mistakes you can make is spending a lot of time with people who aren't interested in improving their skills or performance. It's the ones who are interested who deserve your time and energy.

LESSON 15

Pulling It All Together

In this lesson, you'll review the performance appraisal process. You'll also receive some checklists that will help make your performance appraisals more successful.

PERFORMANCE APPRAISAL—A PROCESS

I've covered a lot of ground since the introduction, where General Electric CEO Jack Welch says that he spends his time on people, not strategy. Now it's time to pull everything together into a cohesive performance appraisal process.

I'd like to begin by emphasizing the word *process*. Too many leaders view performance appraisals as projects that require attention once or twice a year. This approach explains most of the failings that occur with performance appraisals.

Performance appraisals are ongoing processes that encompass

- An evaluation of the employee's current performance.

- Goals for improving that performance.

- The definition of future rewards for achieving the goals.

- Feedback systems that allow both the leader and the employee to monitor her performance.

- Periodic meetings between the leader and the employee to discuss the employee's progress toward her goals.

- Corrective action when the employee is struggling to achieve her goals.

Each and every one of these components is vital to performance improvement.

- Employees can't improve their performance unless they know their current level of performance.

- Their goals must be quantifiable so that they can measure their success.

- Knowing what rewards to expect enhances their interest in achieving goals.

- The ability to monitor their progress helps the employees remain focused on their goals.

- Periodic meetings increase the likelihood that the employees will use the feedback systems to monitor their own progress.

- The requirement that employees report their results in periodic meetings reduces the likelihood they'll miss their targets. After all, no one likes to admit failure.

- Corrective action is best determined in discussions that identify the reasons for the employees' failure to meet goals.

On the surface, this process appears to require a great deal of time. That doesn't have to be the case.

TIP

> My experience has been that every hour I invest in these activities saves me at least three to four hours of follow-up, problem solving, and scrambling to meet deadlines.

TIME COMMITMENTS

The initial appraisal meetings can be accomplished in a couple of hours per employee. In these meetings you'll identify the current level of performance, establish improvement goals, create tracking systems, and define future rewards. If you handle the rest of the process well, your subsequent appraisal meetings can be completed in as little as a 45 minutes to an hour.

The next investment in time comes in the form of establishing feedback mechanisms. In the initial meeting you identified the measures to be used when you established the goals. All that's left is to put a reporting system in place. Keep it simple!

As I discussed in Lesson 13, "Feedback Systems and Recognition Programs," the results can be posted on a bulletin board, a white board, or the intranet. The medium isn't as important as the message. Just make sure that both you and your employees are able to monitor their performance from the same system.

Once the system is in place, the tracking and reporting should take only a few minutes per day. Often you can assign this task to someone other than the employee being evaluated. Don't feel compelled to do all the work yourself.

TIP

> If your tracking and reporting systems are complex, you probably have the wrong measures. Your best results come when you focus on activities where the results are easy to measure.

Your only other time commitment in this phase is the time you spend creating fun ways to celebrate your employees' success. The interesting thing is that the more successful your employees become at managing themselves, the more time you have for these activities.

The time invested in periodic meetings is determined by the success of the employee. If the employee stays on target, you need only spend five minutes a week or a half-hour per month discussing their progress. A few minutes spent letting them know how that you care about their success and that you're happy to see them succeeding means a lot to them. It can also save you countless hours of supervision.

If the employee isn't succeeding, you'll need to spend more time meeting with her to help her get back on track. If that doesn't occur within a reasonable time frame, use the approach outlined in Lesson 14, "You Can't Win 'Em All," and place the responsibility for her future employment where it belongs, in her hands.

ESTABLISHING TIME FRAMES FOR CORRECTIVE ACTION

What's a reasonable time frame? That depends on the goal. If the task is one that should be accomplished in days, then a reasonable time frame is a week. If it should be accomplished in a few weeks, then a month is a reasonable time frame. You'll notice that I am allowing a little more time than should be needed. There are two reasons for this.

First, I want to give the employee every opportunity to succeed. I am truly interested in her success. There are times when the likelihood of success is enhanced by taking pressure out of the situation. In this instance, I'm removing time pressure.

Second, if the employee chooses not to take corrective action, I don't want her to have the opportunity to say that I established unrealistic time frames. Quite the opposite, I want to be able to demonstrate that I gave her every opportunity to succeed.

If the employee fails, I want the failure to clearly be her failure. If termination is warranted, I want the decision to be viewed as her decision. How? By allowing her failure to become evidence of her lack of desire to continue her employment. I'm not going to waste my time trying to help someone who won't help herself.

You can see that it doesn't require much of your time to assure the success of your appraisals. In fact, time spent wisely in the interval between appraisals can actually reduce the time you spend in future appraisal meetings. Since your employees are going to be more successful using this approach, your future meetings will also be more enjoyable. Now that's a winning combination: less time, more enjoyment.

One last reminder: Make sure that the language you use reflects current success and increased success. That way your employees won't feel that they're being criticized.

Now that you have an overview of the system, let's look at some checklists that'll help you keep the appraisal process on track.

TIP

Some people view checklists as a crutch to help someone with a poor memory. I view checklists as a tool to help me develop and maintain good work habits. I hope you'll adopt the latter view.

DAILY CHECKLIST

❑ Have the feedback systems been updated?

❑ Have I reviewed the feedback?

❑ Have I publicly recognized all achievements?

❑ Have I honored my commitments to periodic meetings today?

❑ Did I earn my employees' trust today?

❑ Were there any performance problems that I neglected to address today?

❑ Are there any concerns that I have that I haven't expressed to my employees?

❑ Are there any expectations that I haven't communicated to my employees today?

WEEKLY CHECKLIST

❑ Have I spent at least a few minutes with every employee this week?

❑ Have I recognized every employee at least once this week?

❑ Did I find some interesting ways to celebrate my employees' success this week?

❑ Do any of my employees appear to be behind schedule in achieving their goals?

❑ For the employees who are falling behind, did I take time to discuss their problems and help them get back on track?

❑ Are any of these employees exhibiting signs of lack of interest or boredom with their work?

❑ If an employee is developing a morale problem, did I discuss it with her?

❑ If I've had more than two discussions with an employee about morale, did I employ the approach defined in Lesson 14 and place the employee's future employment in her hands?

CAUTION

Occasionally failing to accomplish an item on the checklist does not make you a bad leader. It simply means that you're human. Just don't allow yourself to get in the habit of skipping items.

These simple checklists will help you stay focused on your primary responsibility, which is developing your people. They also help your employees remain focused on their goals, which assures improved performance. When your employees are more productive the company benefits as well. Everyone wins, which is the way it should be.

The performance appraisal is one of the most powerful tools available to you. Use it wisely, and it'll simplify your life and help you become recognized as master at developing people.

THE 30-SECOND RECAP

- Businesses are always looking for leaders.

- People who have the ability to develop leaders are rare.

- The performance appraisal will help you develop the skills necessary to become one of those people.

- When that happens, you become invaluable; you can write your own ticket. My wish for you is that you achieve that level of success.

Appendix A

Glossary

360° feedback   A performance appraisal system that elicits input from an employee's boss, peers, and subordinates.

activity-based costing   The process of assigning costs to the various activities involved in offering a product or service to your customers.

communication triggers   Deadlines, events, or results that cause you and your employee to get together to discuss performance.

continuous improvement   This phrase describes the goal of becoming better at what we do every day of our lives.

cost-benefit analysis   The process of comparing the cost of achieving a goal against the benefit to be gained by its achievement.

current performance   The result you're getting today.

cycle time   The amount of time needed to complete an activity.

development plan   This is a detailed approach designed to help an employee develop new skills.

downsizings   These are significant reductions in a company's workforce designed to cut costs.

emotional agreement   A level of agreement in which the agreeing party is inspired to act.

employee retention   The ability to keep valued employees.

flat organizations   Companies that have fewer than four layers of management.

grievance   A formal complaint which is filed by a union employee, and supported by the union, against the employer.

Internet   The Internet (also known as the World Wide Web) is a technology that allows people and companies throughout the world to connect with one another using their computers.

intranet   This is a network technology similar to the Internet that has been constructed by a company for its own benefit. Usually access to a company's intranet is limited to its employees, customers, and vendors.

just-in-time inventory   This is a system designed to bring in only those materials needed for the current day's production. This allows the company to minimize its storage and handling costs.

logical agreement   The acceptance of the rationale behind your idea by another person.

mass customization   This is the process of customizing your product or service to meet the individual customer's needs while serving thousands of customers every day.

master people developer   Someone who is expert at helping others develop their skills and improve their performance.

mean   In a numerical sequence, the number that has an equal number of values before and after it. In the sequence 3, 5, 7, 9, 11, seven is the mean.

mentor   A wise and trusted advisor.

merger   This occurs when two companies combine operations to form one company.

micromanagement   A managerial style in which the manager controls minute details of the effort.

outsource   To contract for services rather than have employees perform the work.

performance appraisal   The act of evaluating an employee's performance or the form used in that evaluation.

process mapping   A method used to examine the effectiveness of the approach currently used in completing a task.

protégé   The person being mentored (see *mentor*).

recruiting   The process of locating, evaluating, and hiring new employees.

return on average capital employed   A financial ratio that compares profits generated to assets employed. The ratio is often adjusted to reflect that some of the assets are financed by noninterest-bearing debt.

rework   The process of redoing a task to correct an error.

sandwich generation   People in their 50s and 60s who find themselves caring for three generations: themselves, their children, and their parents.

value   That combination of quality and price that allows the buyer to feel that she's getting more than she is paying for.

Appendix B
Further Readings

Blanchard, Ken, and Sheldon Bowles. *Raving Fans: A Revolutionary Approach to Customer Service.* New York: William Morrow & Co., May 1993.

Furtwengler, Dale. *Making The Exceptional Normal.* St. Louis: Peregrine Press, November 1997.

Kaplan, Robert, and David Norton. *The Balanced Scorecard.* Boston: Harvard Business School Press, 1996.

Kelly, Patrick. *Faster Company.* New York: John Wiley & Sons, Inc., 1998.

Kirkpatrick, Donald L. *Evaluating Training Programs: The Four Levels.* San Francisco: Berrett-Koehler Publishers, Inc., 1998.

INDEX

SYMBOLS

360-degree feedback, appraisal techniques, 77-78

A

activity-based costing, performance measure, 10-11
admitting errors, employees, 106
alternative appraisal approach, performance appraisals, 79-80
appraisals, performance
    approaches,
        emotional constraints,
        112-114
        employee-directed/
        lender-directed,
        111-112
        logical agreements,
        111-112
        performance appraisals,
        94-95
    components, 140-141
    forms, 75-77
    meetings, 129-130
    problems, 129-130

process
    building trust, 101-102
    performance appraisals,
    140-141
reviews, 79-80
style, 94
tasks, 84
techniques
    360-degree feedback,
    77-78
    employee performance,
    98-99
    performance appraisals,
    77-78, 94-95
attitude problems, performance appraisals, 129-130

B

Balanced Scorecard, The, book, 12-13, 150
base pay, annual increases, 49
books
    Balanced Scorecard,The,
    12-13, 150
    Evaluating Training Programs:
    The Four Levels, 125, 150

Faster Company, 150
*Making the Exceptional
    Normal*, 150
*Raving Fans: A Revolutionary
    Approach to Customer
    Service*, 29, 150

C

candor and disagreement, perfor-
    mance appraisals, 96
checklists (performance appraisals)
    daily, 144
    weekly, 145
comment section, performance
    appraisals, 67-68
communication
    co-workers, 52-53
    cooperative, 57-58
    dictatorial, 57-58
    emotional reactions and tech-
        niques, 60-61
    employee respect, 57
    employees, 52-53, 60-61
    encouraging success, 64
    feelings, 57
    incomplete communications,
        54-55
    listening, 55-56
    moods, 58-60
    questions, 55-56
    parental, 57-58
    performance appraisals,
        8, 42-45, 61-63, 82
    skills
        *performance appraisals, 1
        performance criteria,
            74-75*
    submissive, 57-58
    tips, 53-54
    tone of voice, employees,
        60-61

triggers
    *performance appraisals,
        61-63, 82*
    *performance improvement,
        117-119*
companies
    costs, 30-32
    flatter organizations, 37
    improvement, performance
        appraisals, 45-47
    learning, 38
    outsource, 30-32
compensation
    annual increases, 49
    decisions, performance
        appraisals, 1
    incentive programs, 50-51
    inflationary increases, 49
    organizations, large and small,
        49-50
    packages, 12
    programs, evaluations, 6-7
    rewards, improvement
        measures, 114-116
    value proposition, 45
compensation and performance,
    employee understanding, 48-49
confidence problems, employees,
    132-135
cooperation, communication, 57-58
corrective actions, performance
    appraisals, 143-144
credit and collection, 124-125
critical performances, performance
    appraisals, 84-91
current performance
    goals, 15-17
    performance appraisals,
        141-143
    performance measurements, 15
customers
    orders, mass customization,
        2-3

services
external and internal, 3
value criteria, 4

D

daily measurements, tracking programs, 13-15
deadlines
improvement measures, 114
performance improvement, 117-119
development plan
employees, mentors, 25-26
skill development, 26-27
dictatorial communication, 57-58
disenchanted employees, employee productivity, 48
downsizings, 132-133

E

education, employees, 132-133
effective listening, communication, 55-56
effective productivity, employee satisfaction, 34
effective questions, communication, 55-56
elements, performance appraisals, 1
emotional agreements
appraisal approaches, 111-112
performance appraisals, managers, 108-111
performance measures, 112-114
emotional commitment, improvement measures, 112-114
emotional constraints, appraisal approach, 112-114

emotional reactions and techniques, communication, 60-61
employee-directed appraisal approaches, 111-112
employees
absenteeism, 32-33
accomplishments, 102-103
admitting errors, 106
attitudes
employee satisfaction, 5-6
performance criteria, 73-74
company costs, 30-32
confidence problems, 132-135
contributions, 102-103
creativity, performance criteria, 74
development
employee skills, 4-5
mentoring tips, 4-5
performance appraisals, 1
differences, employee satisfaction, 40-41
dissatisfaction, employee absenteeism, 32-33
education, 132-133
feelings, 104-105
initiative, performance criteria, 75
interests, exploring questions (mentors), 22-24
job security, 132-133
low self-esteem, 132-135
micromanagement, 106
morale problems, 131-135
participation
employee satisfaction, 38-39
performance appraisals, 80-82
performance goals, 92
peers, 104-105

performance
appraisal techniques,
98-99
improvement, 133-134
problems, 103-104
perks, continuous improvement,
17-18
personal growth, 130-131
perspective, performance
appraisals, 80-82
planning, performance criteria,
75-77
professional growth, 130-134
productivity, disenchanted
employees, 48
recognition tips, 102-103
respect, communication, 57
retention, 30-32
satisfaction
effective productivity, 34
employee attitudes, 5-6
employee differences,
40-41
employee participation,
38-39
enthusiasm, 35
growth opportunities, 37
job satisfaction, 5-6
money, 35-36
performance appraisals, 1,
5-6
productivity and quality,
34
public recognition, 39-40
security, 40
training and development,
38
variety, 36
self-confidence, performance
appraisals, 93-94
skills, 4-5
success, 102
superiority, 104-105
tone, communication, 60-61

trust violations, 102
understanding, compensation
and performance, 48-49
working situations, 133
enthusiasm, employee satisfaction,
35
Evaluating Training Programs: The
Four Levels, book, 125, 150
evaluations
compensation programs, 6-7
employees, mentors, 21-22
process, performance criteria,
72
examining employees, strengths and
interests, 24-25
expectations, raising, 47
external customers, customer
service, 3

F

Faster Company, book, 150
feedback
measures
marketing, 119-122
quantifiable measurements,
122-123
systems
feedback tips, 126-127
job performance, 136-138
performance improvement,
117-119
quantifiable measurements,
marketing, 122
recognition programs,
127-128
sales management,
122-123
tips, feedback systems, 126-127
feelings, communication, 57
finance groups, 126-127
flatter organizations, companies, 37
formal complaint, grievances, 33

G

goals
    current performance, 15-17
    improvements, performance
        measurements, 15-17
    production services, 12-13
    unrealistic, performance mea-
        surements, 15-17
    well-balanced, 12-13
grievances, 33
growth opportunities, employee sat-
    isfaction, 37

H

happy employees
    benefits, 29
    employee retention, 30-32
human resources, 125

I

improvements
    employee perks, 17-18
    job satisfaction, 17-18
    measures
        compensation rewards,
        114-116
        deadlines, 114
        emotional commitment,
        112-114
        performance measures,
        17-18, 112-114
    opportunities, discussing
        strengths, 110-111
incentive compensation, pay pro-
    grams, 50-51
incomplete communications, 54-55
inflationary increases, compensation,
    49

initial appraisals, 141-143
internal customers, customer service,
    3
interpersonal skills, performance cri-
    teria, 73

J

jobs
    changes, 136-138
    knowledge, mentors, 20
    performance, 136-138
    satisfaction
        continuous improvement,
        17-18
        employee satisfaction, 5-6
        job changes, 136-138
        performance measures,
        114-116
        performance problems,
        136-138
    security, employees, 132-133
joint decision techniques, perfor-
    mance appraisals, 98-99

L

language, performance appraisals, 95
large organizations, compensation,
    49-50
leader-directed, appraisal approaches,
    111-112
learning companies, 38
listening, effective communication,
    55-56
logical agreement
    appraisal approaches, 111-112
    performance appraisals, man-
        agers, 108-111
low self-esteem, employees, 132, 135

M

Making the Exceptional Normal, book, 150
managers
    building trust, 107
    emotional and logical agreements, performance appraisals, 108-111
    micromanagers, 106
    words and actions, 107
marketing
    feedback, 119-122
    public awareness, 120-122
    team, performance improvement, 120-122
mass customization, 2-3
measuring performance, 9-12
mentors, 19
    development plans, 25-26
    employees, 22-26
    evaluating employee strengths, 21-22
    evaluating questions, 21-22
    examining employees, strengths and interests, 24-25
    job knowledge, 20
    performance appraisals, employee interests, 22-24
    personal development, 20-21
    reassignment plan, 24-25
    tips, employee development, 4-5
    trustworthy, 20-21
mergers, 132-133
micromanagement, 106
micromanagers, 106
money, employee satisfaction, 35-36
moods, communication, 58-60
morale problems, employees, 131-135
motivational rewards, compensation programs, 6-7

N

neutral performance appraisals, 84-91
numeric measures
    averages, mean, and numeric sequences, 65-67
    performance appraisals, 65-67
    performance criteria, 69-70

O

organizational skills, performance criteria, 75-77
outsources, companies and employee retention, 30-32

P

parental communication, 57-58
past performances, performance measurements, 48
pay programs, incentive compensation, 50-51
peers, 104-105
perception of quality, 4
performance appraisals, 84-91, 141-143
    accepting responsibility, 97
    alternative appraisal approach, 79-80
    approaches, 94-95
    aspects, 70-72
    attitude problems, 129-130
    avoiding employee comparisons, 105
    candor and disagreement, 96
    celebrate accomplishments, 96
    checklists, 143-144
    comment sections, 67-68
    communication, 1, 8, 42-45, 61-63, 82

compensation, 1, 6-7
components, 140-141
corrective actions, 143-144
criteria, 69-77
critical performances, 84-91
criticizing privately, 103-104
current performances,
    141-143
daily checklists, 144
discussing improvement oppor-
    tunities, 110-111
elements, 1
employees
    comfort, 92
    development, 1
    interests, mentors, 22-24
    participation, 80-82
    satisfaction, 1, 5-6
    self-confidence, 93-94
    skills, 4-5
    perspectives, 80-82
encouraging performance,
    84-91
evaluations, 79, 105
feedback, 92-93
forms, 65, 75-77
goals, 15-17, 92, 141-143
improvements
    communication triggers,
        117-119
    deadlines, 117-119
    employees, 133-134
    feedback systems,
        117-119
    marketing team, 120, 122
    performance appraisals
        and measurements, 1-2
    progress reports, 117-119
    teaching employees,
        48-49
initial appraisal, 141-143
joint decision techniques,
    98-99

judging performance, 96
language, 95
managers, 108-111
measurements, 9-12, 15
    activity-based costing,
        10-11
    company improvement,
        45-47
    compensation package, 12
    continuous improvement,
        17-18
    current performance, 15
    end results, 9
    expectations, 47
    goals, 15-17
    improvements, 1-2,
        15-17, 112-114
    job satisfaction, 114-116
    performances, 1-3, 48
    process mapping, 10-11
    quantifiable measures,
        11-12
    results, 9-10
    terms, 1-2
    tracking programs, 13-14
    value questions, 45-47
meetings, 92, 129-130
neutral performance, 84-91
numeric measures, 65-67
problems
    employees, 103-104
    job satisfaction, 136-138
process, 101-102, 140-141
recognition, 127-128
respect, 97
reviews, 79-80
salary reviews, 42-44, 97-98,
    129-130
style, 94
tasks, 84
techniques, 77-78, 94-95
termination, 143-144
tracking systems, 141, 143
weekly checklists, 145

personal development, mentors,
20-21
personal growth, employees,
130-131
process mapping, performance measure, 10-11
production, 123-124
publishing, daily measurement
tracking programs, 14-15
services, goals, 12-13
productivity, employee satisfaction,
34
professional growth, employees,
130-134
progress reports, performance
improvement, 117-119
public awareness, marketing,
120-122
public recognition, employee satisfaction, 39-40

Q

quality performance, measurements,
3
quantifiable measurements
feedback, 122-123
performance measure, 11-12
questions, effective communication,
55-56

R

*Raving Fans: A Revolutionary
Approach to Customer Service*,
book, 29, 150
reassignment plans, mentors, 24-25
recognition programs, feedback systems, 127-128
recognition tips, employees,
102-103

S

salary reviews, performance
appraisals, 42-44, 97-98, 129-130
sales, 122-123
sandwich generation, employee
absenteeism, 32-33
security, employee satisfaction, 40
skill development plans, 26-27
small organizations, compensation,
49-50
speed techniques, mass customization, 2-3
submissive communication, 57-58
success, encouraging, 64

T

termination, performance appraisals,
143-144
tracking programs (systems), 13-15,
141-143
training and development, employee
satisfaction, 38
trust violations, employees, 102

U-V

value
customer service, 4
proposition, compensation, 45
questions, performance measurements, 45-47
variety, employee satisfaction, 36
violations, grievances, 33

W-Z

words and actions, managers, 107

More than two million copies previously sold!

Master the skills you need in ten minutes or less.

New & improved look!

All new content!

Ideal as a mini-management series!

Conducting a Job Interview
ISBN: 0-02-863...
Price: $10.95
Available
December 200...

Leadership,
Second Edition
ISBN: 0-02-863611-2
Price: $10.95
Available July 2000

Managing Your Time
ISBN: 0-02-863886-7
Price: $10.95
Available
April 2000

Stress Management
ISBN: 0-02-863995-2
Price: $10.95
Available
December 2000

Project Management
ISBN: 0-02-863966-9
Price: $10.95
Available
August 2000

Motivating People,
Second Edition
ISBN: 0-02-863...
Price: $10.95
Available
April 2000

Business
Presentations
ISBN: 0-02-863965-0
Price: $10.95
Available
September 2000

Effective Business Writing
ISBN: 0-02-864031-4
Price: $10.95
Available
March 2001

Customer Service
ISBN: 0-02-864067-5
Price: $10.95
Available
March 2001

Performance Reviews
ISBN: 0-02-86...
Price: $10.95
Available
October 2000

Macmillan USA